THE BEST OF

Taste

THE BEST OF

Taste

Mouthwatering menus from some of
the world's best cooks

EDITED BY MARIE-PIERRE MOINE

Wine Notes by Robin Young

Macdonald Orbis

A Macdonald Orbis BOOK

© Focus Magazines 1989

First Published in Great Britain in 1989
by Macdonald & Co (Publishers) Ltd
London & Sydney

A member of Maxwell Pergamon Publishing
Corporation plc

British Library Cataloguing in Publication
Data

The Best of Taste.
    1. Food. Party dishes. Recipes
    I. Moine, Marie-Pierre
    II. Taste magazine
    641.5'68

ISBN 0-356-17526-X

Filmset by SB Datagraphics, Colchester

Printed and bound in Italy by L.E.G.O.

Editors: Rosamond Man, Coralie Dorman,
Sarah Chapman
Designer: Sheila Volpe
Art Director: Bobbie Colgate-Stone

Macdonald & Co (Publishers) Ltd
Greater London House
Hampstead Road
London NW1 7QX

CONTENTS

A few words about *Taste* magazine. It was created early in 1986 for the many people who are enthusiastic about food and wine: it simply happens to be their hobby, and they enjoy cooking, eating and entertaining. From choosing the bread they eat for breakfast to picking a good olive oil, and experimenting with coconut milk recipes, *Taste* readers care about what they eat and what they give their family and friends to eat. Their idea of bliss is to spend a day in the kitchen. *Entertaining with Taste* is an experience to be enjoyed, from mulling over the menu to sharing the finished dishes with the guests and, yes, occasionally, basking a little in their compliments.

This selection of menus from *Taste* magazine is for people who love both entertaining and variety — who love to suit their menus not just to the season, but also to the budget, the guests, the time available, and the degree of formality or informality of the occasion. One thing I have found somewhat disappointing about many a collection of dinner party menus is the fact that they are written by a single author, desperately trying to drum up original ideas for menu number nineteen . . . not an easy job. The menus in *Entertaining with Taste* are by different writers — all exciting, gifted cooks and top names in the food world. They were encouraged to do their own thing and each asked to create a menu that truly reflects what they enjoy preparing at home for their own guests — not to seek originality at all costs. The fact that they are very different people with very different personalities, catering for all kinds of occasions — casual supper, weekend brunch, Easter lunch, or chic dinner — takes care of the variety. The *Taste* team was firm about three points: the menus had to be feasible and they weren't to break the bank. For each there was to be a realistic timetable to help plan the meal. A harassed, behind-schedule cook can't hope to relax at her or his own party. The *Taste* approach is that a good time should be had by all, and that definitely includes the hostess or host.

Another important aspect of entertaining is, of course, finding wines that will do the various dishes justice! Again, the accent is on variety: the writers chose wines they liked for their menus and *Taste*'s Wine Editor Robin Young added his comments and suggestions (occasionally agreeing to disagree with the writer's choice). The idea was not to dictate, but to point readers in the right direction, and give them alternatives. Letters regularly remind me that well-stocked wine racks are not always within reach locally in stores and off-licences. There is nothing more infuriating and off-putting than not finding a very specifically recommended wine and being at a loss as to what else to buy!

I would like to thank Rosamond Man and the *Taste* team and contributors, past and present, for their hard work and help.

Happy entertaining: I very much hope you will enjoy this collection of menus and will feel inspired to share its contents with friends and family.

Marie-Pierre Moine

SPRING

*F*or our ancestors, spring was always the most welcomed of the seasons. After months of dry salted meat, then the Lenten weeks with no meat at all, the new season's lamb was a most eagerly awaited event: a luxury with which to celebrate Easter and the arrival of spring. Josceline Dimbleby and Clare Ferguson suggest two quite different — and highly original — treatments for this most delicious of meats.

Young, fresh vegetables, too, were much looked forward to: in Victorian times, the sight of the nettle-sellers in Covent Garden market was the first sign that spring was on the way. As the season progresses, so does the choice become abundant: baby carrots and turnips, mange-touts, pencil-slim leeks, salad leaves in variety. Give vegetables then a place of honour, as does Coralie Dorman, with her tempura of vegetables and dipping sauce. She has taken advantage, too, of the fish that is now so plentiful with her delicate and unusual main course — hake with oyster sabayon. Fay Maschler's Sunday lunch echoes the fish theme, with crab mayonnaise on shrimp crackers and prawns piri-piri to start, while cleverly catering for any chill spring winds with that lovely Italian classic, *bollito misto*, a dish of hot boiled meats — light but warming.

Continuing the mood is Antonio Carluccio's menu, reflecting, too, the Italian principle of simple cooking with the freshest of ingredients; fat fresh scallops, tender young spinach leaves, plump spring chickens. As the days grow warmer and longer, Lisa Kinsman gives a hint of the plethora of delicacies to come, with her seafood choices of fresh crab, monkfish and squid, followed by an extravaganza of fruits served with floating islands encased in clouds of finely spun sugar. A fitting tribute to spring — and a welcome to summer.

Josceline Dimbleby

EASTER LUNCH

Herald the coming of spring with fresh seasonal flavours — Josceline Dimbleby's lunch menu is perfect for an Easter celebration

---

Scallop and avocado salad

Marinated lamb with wild mushroom sauce
Aubergine purée with pine nuts
Sautéed gingered potatoes
Green salad with primroses, or lightly cooked green vegetable

---

Chocolate and orange egg bombe

Easter is the light at the end of the long winter tunnel. Even if it is still cold and muddy on Easter Sunday there is hope in the bursting buds, fresh green grass and longer days. At Christmas, exhausted after the build-up, you have the worst of the winter yet to face. Easter is a more spontaneous celebration, and heralds the pleasures of spring.

We are nearly always in south Devon for Easter, which seems an especially good place to be: the hedgerows are massed with primroses, often with violets peeping through. Primroses and violets are edible, so if you make a cake try decorating it with flowers instead of chicks. You can also use primrose heads in a green salad.

From left to right: marinated lamb, green salad with primroses, aubergine purée, wild mushroom sauce, chocolate and orange egg bombe

COUNTDOWN

The day before

• *Make the chocolate ice cream and freeze it.*

• *Make the orange custard, put it inside the frozen bombe and freeze until firm.*

• *Finish with the reserved chocolate ice cream and freeze.*

• *Marinate the lamb and leave it in a cool place or in the refrigerator.*

In the morning

• *Defrost the scallops, if using frozen.*

• *Weigh the lamb and calculate the cooking time; bring it to room temperature.*

Two hours before lunch

• *Marinate the scallops in lemon juice, cover and chill.*

• *Soak the mushrooms for the sauce.*

• *Toast the pine nuts for the aubergine purée.*

• *Steam the potatoes and set aside.*

• *Heat the oven to 190C/375F/ gas 5.*

About one hour before

• *Cook the lamb and start the mushroom and tomato sauce.*

• *Prepare the green salad, if using, and put it in the refrigerator.*

About 30 minutes before

• *Prepare the aubergine purée, cover and keep warm in the bottom of the oven.*

• *Sauté the potatoes and spices and keep warm.*

• *Prepare the turnips for the scallop salad, chop the dill and make the vinaigrette dressing.*

• *Release the bombe from its mould on to a serving plate and put it back in the freezer.* ▶

When planning a festive meal, Easter, unlike Christmas, has no rules that you are bound to obey. At a farm near us in Devon, I used to buy large capons which had a lot of flavour — a turkey is no alternative, as it is too similar to Christmas food. But I think the best treat for Easter is fresh English lamb.

A leg of lamb is easier to carve than a shoulder but, being lean meat, it has less flavour. The answer is to marinate it, as in the following recipe. A delicate fish dish is nearly always good before lamb. I have a passion for scallops so I have chosen them to start this special meal.

Both the aubergine purée and the spiced sautéed potatoes which accompany the lamb are wonderful dishes in themselves, so if any member of the family is a vegetarian, as one of my daughters is, they will certainly not feel hard done by. For a touch of green I would serve either a green salad with primroses, steamed or lightly boiled broccoli or French beans that are still bright green and slightly crunchy. Don't cook the vegetables in advance, simply prepare them and cook them at the last minute. They need only about 5 minutes' cooking, and this won't be difficult to cope with as the rest of the meal will be in hand.

For the finale I'm afraid I have been unable to resist chocolate — a heavenly iced chocolate and orange surprise designed specially for Easter Day. However indulgent the family have been with their Easter eggs during the morning, I don't think they will be able to resist this kind of egg.

I think it would be nice to serve both a white and a red wine with this meal. With the scallops I'd serve a Californian Chardonnay or else a good Sauvignon that is aromatic and slightly smoky. If you feel both festive and generous champagne would go very well.

As the lamb course has strong and exciting flavours you will need a fruity, robust wine. A Californian Cabernet Sauvignon or a Shiraz would be ideal. There is a delicious Australian Shiraz called Sea View Coonawarra.

I don't feel that the rich ice cream needs sweet wine but if you want one, try Sauternes.

SCALLOP AND AVOCADO SALAD

You need only the lightest of first courses for an Easter meal, and this pretty scallop salad is a perfect appetiser. Little scallops, called queens, are stocked frozen by most fishmongers; if you are lucky you'll find fresh ones. There is no need to cook the scallops as they taste better if you simply soak them in lemon juice.

SERVES 6

700g/1½lb small scallops (queens) — thawed if frozen, drained and patted dry

juice of 3 large lemons

freshly ground black pepper and salt

500g/1lb baby turnips (navets)

bunch of fresh dill (or about 4 teaspoons dried dill)

extra virgin olive oil

3 large avocados

1. Put the scallops into a bowl and pour over the lemon juice to cover them. Sprinkle with black pepper, cover the bowl and leave in the refrigerator for at least 30 minutes.

2. Wash the turnips. Cook in boiling salted water for 5-10 minutes or until bite-tender. Refresh under cold water. Discard the root sections, then cut the turnips across into thin circles.

3. Chop the dill finely if using fresh. Pour the lemon juice off the scallops into a jug and then add about double the amount of olive oil, and seasoning, to form a vinaigrette. Mix the chopped dill with the scallops.

4. Just before serving, cut the avocados in half, remove the stones and peel; slice thinly. Arrange them alternately

Countdown (continued)

Just before the first course
• *Slice the avocados and arrange with the turnips on a plate. Finish the dish with the scallops and vinaigrette.*

After the first course
• *Finish the sauce, while leaving the lamb to 'rest' on top of the stove before carving.*
• *Lightly cook the green vegetable, if using, or garnish the green salad with primroses.*
• *Garnish the aubergine purée and the sautéed potatoes.*

After the main course
• *Remove the bombe from the freezer and decorate.*

with the turnip slices on a shallow circular serving dish, leaving a space for the scallops in the middle. Spoon in the scallops so that they slightly overlap the avocados and turnips. Spoon the vinaigrette over the whole dish.

Note:
Soaking the scallops in lemon juice 'cooks' the fish as thoroughly as if it had actually been heated. Left to marinate, the citric acid turns the flesh white and firm.

MARINATED LAMB WITH WILD MUSHROOM SAUCE

Marinating meat can improve its flavour and texture, particularly with a lean joint like a leg of lamb. A good sauce also transforms a roast: although dried ceps (*porcini*) are quite expensive, their flavour is intense and helps makes a wonderful sauce.

SERVES 6

1 leg lamb, about 2kg/4½lb
lemon slices and sprigs of thyme to garnish
FOR THE MARINADE
juice and zest of 1 orange
juice of 1 lemon
1 teaspoon ground mace
1 tablespoon tomato purée
2 tablespoons extra virgin olive oil
salt and black pepper
small bunch of fresh thyme
FOR THE SAUCE
10g packet dried ceps (porcini)
1 tablespoon extra virgin olive oil
1 large garlic clove, finely chopped
400g/14oz can chopped tomatoes
juice of 1 large orange
salt and black pepper
150ml/¼pt double cream

1. To prepare the marinade: place the orange zest in a bowl with the orange and lemon juices. Add the ground mace, tomato purée, olive oil, a little salt and plenty of freshly ground black pepper. Pull the leaves off the thyme, add half to the marinade mixture and press the remaining leaves into 3 or 4 deep incisions in the leg of lamb. Place the joint on a large piece of foil and smear the orange and tomato marinade over it.
2. Enclose the lamb in the foil and put it in the refrigerator or a cool place for several hours or until the next day. Bring the joint to room temperature for an hour or two before you start to cook it.
3. Soak the ceps (broken up a little if they are in large pieces) in tepid water; change the water 2-3 times, and leave for at least an hour. Heat the oven to 190C/375F/gas 5. Unwrap the lamb and cook it in a roasting pan in the centre of the oven for 33 minutes per kg/15 minutes per lb for pale-pink lamb, or 39-44 minutes per kg/18-20 minutes per lb for just a hint of pink.
4. Meanwhile, make the sauce. Heat the olive oil in a heavy-based saucepan. Add the chopped garlic. Stir in the tomatoes and the orange juice. Season with salt and plenty of freshly ground black pepper. Now add the drained soaked mushrooms, bring them to the boil, then cover the saucepan and simmer gently for about ¾-1 hour.
5. When the lamb is cooked, let it rest on top of the stove for about 10 minutes before carving. Add the double cream to the sauce and bubble for a minute or two. Pour off any excess fat from the roasting pan, and pour the juices and any scrapings of residue into the sauce. Check the sauce for seasoning and pour it into a sauceboat. Serve the lamb garnished with the lemon slices and sprigs of fresh thyme.

AUBERGINE PURÉE WITH PINE NUTS

This purée of aubergine with soft white cheese is excellent with roast lamb. The subtle smoky flavour of the purée is achieved by grilling whole aubergines until their skins are burnt black and cracked.

SERVES 6

1kg/2lb large aubergines
50g/2oz butter, softened
100g/4oz full-fat soft cheese with garlic
¼ teaspoon cayenne pepper, plus extra to garnish
salt
25-50g/1-2oz pine nuts
coriander leaves to garnish

1. Put the whole, unpeeled aubergines under the hottest grill for approximately 15-20 minutes, turning them continuously until they are black all over and the skin has blistered. Holding the hot aubergines in a cloth, break them open and scrape the flesh out into a food processor with a metal spoon. Add the butter and soft cheese and whizz to a smooth purée. Season to taste with cayenne pepper and salt. Spoon the mixture into a warm serving bowl.
2. Heat a small, dry frying pan and add the pine nuts; toss for 1-2 minutes or until toasted dark brown. Scatter the nuts over the aubergine purée, cover the dish with foil and keep it warm in a low oven until ready to eat.
3. Garnish with a sprinkling of cayenne pepper and some fresh coriander leaves.

SAUTÉED GINGERED POTATOES

These potatoes are truly wonderful. In the unlikely event that they are not all eaten, they are also delicious cold. Use a wok or a large frying pan for sautéeing. Red-skinned Desirée potatoes or any with a close texture are particularly good for this recipe.

If you want to cook the potatoes in advance, they will keep warm without spoiling for several hours, but remember to add the parsley and salt only just before serving.

SERVES 6

1kg/2lb large potatoes
2-3 large garlic cloves
5cm/2in piece fresh root ginger
3 tablespoons olive or groundnut oil
25g/1oz butter
3 teaspoons ground cumin
4 teaspoons caraway seeds
freshly ground black pepper
sea salt
bunch of parsley, chopped

1. Scrub the potatoes and slice them into roughly 2.5cm/1in pieces. Steam or boil them until they are just tender — about 10 minutes.
2. Peel the garlic and ginger and chop them finely together. Heat the oil and butter in a large wok or frying pan. Stir in the garlic and ginger, then add the ground cumin and caraway seeds; stir for another minute.

3. Add the potatoes and sauté for about 8 minutes until browned on all sides. Sprinkle them with black pepper. Before serving, stir in a sprinkling of sea salt and chopped parsley and serve in a heated dish.

CHOCOLATE AND ORANGE EGG BOMBE

I think this is one of the most mouth-watering ice creams I have ever made. My idea was that it should look like a chocolate egg with a yolk, but of course a bombe mould is not really egg-shaped.

However, it does look appropriate for Easter and can be decorated with spring flowers or with tiny chocolate eggs at the base and perhaps an Easter chick on the top.

The rich but nevertheless light chocolate ice cream is made with whisked egg whites, and the surprise centre consists of a sharp orange-flavoured custard made with the yolks.

SERVES 6

4 large egg whites
½ teaspoon salt
175g/6oz Demerara sugar
250g/8oz plain chocolate
300ml/½pt double or whipping cream
FOR THE ORANGE CUSTARD
4 egg yolks
finely grated zest of 1 orange
150g/5oz caster sugar
125ml/4fl.oz orange juice
few drops of yellow or orange food colouring (optional)

1. To make the ice cream, whisk the egg whites with the salt until they form soft peaks. Dissolve the Demerara sugar in 8 tablespoons of water over a low heat. Increase the heat to high and boil fiercely for exactly 3 minutes. Now gradually pour the syrup on to the egg whites, whisking all the time at high speed. Continue whisking until the mixture has cooled slightly.
2. Break up the chocolate and put it into the top of a double saucepan or a bowl set over a saucepan of hot, but not boiling, water. Stir until melted, then gradually pour on to the egg-white mixture, whisking all the time.
3. Put the cream into another bowl and whisk until it forms soft peaks. Fold the cream into the chocolate mixture until evenly blended, then pour into a 1-1.5L/ 2-2½pt aluminium bombe mould. Freeze for several hours.
4. Make the orange custard. Whisk the egg yolks until pale, then whisk in the orange zest. Dissolve the sugar in the orange juice over a gentle heat. Increase the heat and boil fiercely for 3 minutes. Gradually pour the syrup on to the egg yolks, whisking all the time at high speed. Continue whisking until cooled and thickened. Stir in the food colouring if using.
5. Take the chocolate ice cream from the freezer. Scoop out the centre into a bowl, and put the bowl in the refrigerator to soften. Spoon the orange mixture into the hollow ice cream, and return it to the freezer for about an hour until firm.
6. Spoon the softened ice cream as evenly as possible over the top of the orange centre. Return the bombe to the freezer for several hours.
7. To serve, dip the mould briefly in hot water, invert a plate over the mould and turn the mould and plate over together, giving them a good shake. Lift off the mould and smooth any irregularities with a palette knife dipped in hot water. Finally, put it back in the freezer until you are ready to eat it. Decorate as preferred just before serving.

WINE NOTES

Josceline Dimbleby's suggestions for white wines to accompany the first course are eminently helpful and appropriate, but California Chardonnays do need rather careful selection. They fall into two camps: what the Americans call 'pleasure' wines, and what are known as 'food' wines. The first group are so big, rich and intensely concentrated that they overwhelm most food, while the second are made in a more restrained and classic style. The wine lists, or the staff at the wine companies which list ranges of California wines, will be helpful about pointing you in the right direction.

Australian Shiraz can be a super bargain, often chunky and flavoursomely brambly. Australia, or California, can also provide richly ripe blackcurrant-flavoured Cabernet Sauvignons, which will cost a little more.

Josceline Dimbleby is quite right, of course, that there is no need for dessert wine, and the chocolate and orange ice cream is about as difficult a sweet to match with wine as one could easily conceive.

Still, if you do want a glass of honey-sweet and well-chilled Sauternes, there is no reason why it should not be sipped at ease after the meal has been finished.

Clare Ferguson

SPRING CELEBRATION MENU

Take advantage of brighter days and lighter evenings with Clare Ferguson's delicate menu, reflecting the fresh colours of the new season — with just a touch of late-winter warmth

---

Roasted Stilton with young salad leaves

Prosciutto and garlic-scented spring lamb
Mange-touts with chives
Baby turnips and spring carrots

Green-pine sherbet Chartreuse

Entertaining during the spring months becomes a positive pleasure after winter's darkest days. Brighter evenings make lighter and more delicate food seem sensible and desirable for a celebration of the new season. And as new young vegetables — *primeurs* as the French call them — begin to come on to the market, it is wonderful to make use of their particular charms.

They appear here as a salad of tender young leaves of the endive and lettuce families. Brilliant in hue, delicate in shape and fascinating to the tongue for both texture and taste, the four varieties specified will be sure to provoke interest and enthusiasm, especially with the mellow, classic dressing — which also complements the chilled wine accompaniment.

Stilton or another strong, charac-terful blue cheese served sizzling hot on a chunk of crusty bread, adds unusual deliciousness to this salad. Hot cheese with salad is a combination Parisians have served with panache for years.

Mauve-tinted baby turnips, cooked quite simply but with a new twist, make quite a conversation piece. The freshness and lack of bitterness the technique allows re-establishes the vegetable as a favourite spring treat. Whole baby carrots retain both their nutrients and seasonal charms, while the mange-touts taste almost Oriental — but for the fruitiness of the olive oil in which they cook briefly. Since in all vegetable cuisine one should attempt to preserve goodness as well as texture and taste, I have stressed minimal cooking times and simple but effective presentation.

The perfection of spring lamb could not help but please most palates. I have cooked it in a new way: garlic and nutty Parma ham aromatize it with flavour from within. And there's a superb sauce, the colour of sunshine. The meat should be kept warm for the short time it takes the young vegetables to cook, ensuring tenderness. Garlanded with green mange-touts, the dish would be appropriate for Easter.

If you have a sorbetière — as many people now do — preparing and freezing the sorbet is a last-minute affair. If you don't have one, make it the day before, according to the method I have given, and transfer from freezer to refrigerator to soften one hour before serving.

Wines always play an important part in any festive meal; a good Côtes du Rhône to follow the chilled oloroso served with the salad would be a wise choice.

ROASTED STILTON WITH YOUNG SALAD LEAVES

Four varieties of pretty young leaves in a mellow dressing with sizzling hot, crusty but oozing cheese added as a final flourish at serving time. This delicate dish is noteworthy for its singular flavours and ease of preparation. Do use good French bread.

SERVES 6

1 very fresh baguette
200g/7oz Stilton
100g/4oz frisée (curly endive)
100g/4oz red oak-leaved lettuce
50g/2oz mâche (lamb's lettuce) or young dandelion leaves
50g/2oz radicchio or red trevise endive
FOR THE DRESSING
4 tablespoons walnut, hazelnut or virgin olive oil
1 tablespoon oloroso

1. Heat the oven to 230C/450F/gas 8. Slice the bread on the diagonal to give 6 × 6cm/1½in thick slices. Place a portion of cheese on each and arrange on a baking sheet.

2. Bake towards the top of the oven for about 10 minutes until the bread is crusty and brown and the Stilton is melted, golden and bubbly. Meanwhile, prepare the salad by tearing the cleaned and dried leaves into bite-sized portions and separating the heads of the lamb's lettuce.

3. Put the dressing ingredients into the base of a large salad or mixing bowl. Add the salad leaves but do not stir them into the dressing.

4. Remove the toasted cheese croûtes from the oven. Quickly toss the salad until the leaves glisten with the dressing, then divide it between the 6 serving plates. Place a hot cheese croûte in the centre of each and serve while the Stilton is very hot.

COUNTDOWN

The day before
• *Make sherbet according to recipe, if you do not possess a sorbetière. Keep in freezer.*

Three hours before serving
• *Make incisions in the lamb. Prepare prosciutto and garlic rolls. Insert in joint. Place in roasting pan, cover and keep cool, but not in refrigerator.*
• *Squeeze limes and reserve juice; prepare pineapple and watercress for the sherbet, if you have a sorbetière.*
• *Chill fino sherry, if serving.*

Two hours before
• *Heat oven to 180C/350F/ gas 4. Place lamb in oven (see recipe for preferred cooking times).*
• *Make sherbet mixture, keep cool.*
• *Chill white wine and uncork red.*

One hour before
• *Wash and prepare vegetables; place in cooking pans, cover and keep cool.*
• *Chill oloroso sherry, if serving.*
• *Prepare salad leaves. Add with dressing ingredients to salad bowl. Cover well, refrigerate. Do not toss or stir.*

Half an hour before serving
• *Remove lamb from oven (when cooked to preferred degree of pinkness): keep warm on heated dish. Turn the oven up to 230C/450F/gas 8. Make sauce and keep it warm.*
• *Slice French bread and arrange Stilton portions. Bake.*
• *Toss salad and divide into 6 portions on serving plates.*
• *If using freezer for sherbet, transfer to refrigerator.* ▶

Countdown (continued)

Just before serving
• *Place hot cheese croûtes on salad dishes.*
• *Remove sherry from refrigerator.*
• *Pour sherbet mixture into sorbetière.*

After the starter
• *Cook vegetables carefully. Arrange carrots and turnips, garnish.*
• *Garland lamb with mange-touts.*

After the main course
• *Remove sherbet from sorbetière or refrigerator and beat it. Serve in individual glasses.*

PROSCIUTTO AND GARLIC-SCENTED SPRING LAMB

English leg of lamb becomes a vivacious new dish when served with a saffron and egg sauce and garlic cloves enclosed in 'ribbons' of raw cured Italian ham.

SERVES 6

2kg/4½lb leg of English spring lamb
3-6 slices (depending on size — about 175g/6oz) prosciutto/Parma ham, cut across to make 24 smaller slices
12 garlic cloves, skinned and halved lengthways
2 tablespoons olive oil
freshly ground black pepper
125mg sachet (pinch) powdered saffron
2 egg yolks
100g/4oz curd cheese

1. Heat the oven to 180C/350F/gas 4. Using a small pointed knife, pierce the meat in 24 places evenly over its surface to a depth of 5cm/2in. Roll up each slice of prosciutto, like a cigar. Fold each roll over the end of a teaspoon handle and push into an incision. Two ribbon-like ends of prosciutto should be left just showing. Into each prosciutto-lined incision push half a garlic clove.

2. Put the leg of lamb into a roasting pan and dribble the olive oil over it. Sprinkle generously with freshly ground black pepper. Roast for between 1 hour 20 minutes and 1 hour 40 minutes, according to how pink you like it.

3. Remove from oven and keep warm on a serving dish. Pour off the fat and all but 6 tablespoons of the pan juices.

4. Add the saffron to the reserved juices and stir over a medium heat until dissolved and the liquid is very hot. In a small bowl blend together the egg yolks and curd cheese until smooth. Stir a little of the hot liquid into this and then return to the mixture in the roasting pan, stirring until well blended and just hot. Do not allow the sauce to overheat. Pour into a heated sauceboat. Serve the lamb surrounded with a garland of mange-touts.

MANGE-TOUTS WITH CHIVES

The fresh flavour of mange-touts blends with the musty sweetness of the green oil and the subtle strength of chives.

SERVES 6

500g/1lb young mange-touts, topped and tailed

1 tablespoon virgin olive oil

2 tablespoons snipped fresh chives

1. Wash the mange-touts but do not dry them. Place in a large shallow pan with enough boiling salted water barely to cover the base. Cook, uncovered, very briefly on high heat, tossing occasionally until they are just tender.

2. Add the oil and chives and allow to cook for 1 minute more. Serve piled in a circle around the lamb.

BABY TURNIPS

Blushing mauve-topped young turnips, piled into a pyramid, look vivid and taste splendid because the preparation technique ingeniously allows the inner and outer surfaces to cook at the same pace. Boiling water and steam pass through the centre of each vegetable. After such a brief cooking time, the taste is crunchy fresh, yet they are hot to eat.

SERVES 6

1kg/2lb young turnips (navets) *with stems and roots*

12-15 sprigs flat-leaved parsley

25g/1oz unsalted butter

1. Wash the turnips and, using an apple corer, neatly remove the central stem and root sections and discard.

2. Put into a large shallow frying pan with lid. They should be closely packed together but in one layer. Add boiling water to a depth of 1cm/½in. Cover and cook for 3-5 minutes.

3. Remove to a heated serving dish. Arrange attractively, using the parsley leaves as a central garnish for each. Melt the butter and trickle it over the top. Have rock salt and pepper grinders on the table.

SPRING CARROTS

Baby carrots always cause delight when their bright green stems are left on, indicating their freshness. Cooking time will vary according to their size.

SERVES 6

2 bunches baby carrots, with green stems and tops, or 500g/1lb small carrots

light stock or boiling salted water

1. Scrub the carrots until very clean or, if preferred, use a vegetable peeler to remove the skin, tapering each to a fine point. Wash, leave on the stems and trim these to 2.5cm/1in lengths. Reserve the best leaves.

2. Cook carrots in the boiling stock or water, covered, for 5-8 minutes or until bite tender. Arrange on a heated serving dish in a radiating pattern with some of the reserved tops at the stem ends.

GREEN-PINE SHERBET CHARTREUSE

Here we have a success story of savoury and sweet working well together: pineapple frozen with a peppering of cress as part of the mixture. It provides a fresh taste after the richness of cheese and lamb. Yellow or green Chartreuse adds a scented, aromatic tang.

SERVES 6

175g/6oz caster sugar

225ml/8fl. oz dry white wine

zest and juice of 3 limes

75g/3oz bunch watercress, stalks included, coarsely chopped

500-600g/1-1¼lb fresh pineapple, cut into 1cm/½in chunks (1.1-1.4kg/2½-3lb whole pineapple)

2 tablespoons Chartreuse

4 stems perfect watercress or pineapple slices to serve

1. Stir the sugar and wine together in a pan over gentle heat until the sugar is dissolved, then cool over ice. Stir in the lime zest and juice.

2. Put the chopped watercress into a food processor with the pineapple. Process in short bursts until blended to a speckly rough purée. Add the sugar syrup and blend again.

WINE NOTES

Powerful, tangy Stilton is a surprisingly accommodating cheese for matching with wines. In chilly weather, my favourite would be a dry oloroso sherry—broad, full-bodied, warm and rich. As it turns warmer, good fino can be substituted—Tio Pepe, unusually for a brand leader, consistently does well in blind tastings and can be relied upon. Serve oloroso cool and fino well chilled.

Clare Ferguson's suggestion for the lamb is good Côtes-du Rhône (Château du Grand Moulas and Paul Jaboulet's Parallele 45 are utterly dependable), but I suspect I might prefer a herby, soft young claret to pick up the flavour of the primeur *vegetables, or a young Chianti to highlight the dish's Italianate conception. Chianti Classico Rocca della Macie has been a best buy, vintage after vintage.*

The dessert has two alcoholic ingredients: best leave it there. You might try a bargain sweetie such as Clos St Georges Graves Supérieur, which is delectable even in off-vintages. For port lovers, the emergent star of Oporto is the recently founded house of Churchill Graham, which has quickly made its mark with wines that are characterful, clean and richly tangy.

3. Stir in the liqueur and turn the mixture into a shallow, freezer-proof plastic lidded container, unless you are using a sorbetière. Cover and fast-freeze for 2-2½ hours until mushy. Remove from the freezer and stir from sides to centre. Refreeze for a further 1½-2 hours, beating the mixture once more. Freeze until firm. (Alternatively, use a sorbetière, following the maker's instructions.)

4. Remove from the freezer to the refrigerator about 1 hour before serving. Just before serving stir, using an electric beater on slow speed, or a processor, until a crumbly texture results. Serve in piles or scoops in chilled goblets or on chilled glass dishes, with a few watercress leaves or slices of pineapple.

Coralie Dorman

FRIDAY SUPPER WITH FRIENDS

*The weekend has begun and it's time to relax —
Coralie Dorman's informal meal is quick to
prepare and a pleasure to share*

Tempura vegetables with dipping sauce

Hake with oyster sabayon
Green salad

Fruit in caramel coats

I must admit that entertaining on Fridays is a challenge for me. The temptation to slump, outstretched in a soft armchair with toast and tea, is often overwhelming. However, having spoken to colleagues and esteemed peers, I sense an underlying vein of martyrdom in us professional cooks. Cooking is an act of giving — although we treasure the experience, of course — and must be appreciated. That is why, on a lovely May evening, I have to surround myself by jolly good friends who are willing to put up with my weaknesses and comply by giving their praises generously.

May. What a month. English asparagus, flowers by the fistful, and enough fruit and other vegetables to give us a headache with choosing. I like to sow the seeds of a menu by thinking about what is fresh, what is available, and let it grow when I know these things. Friday's menu should be quick, bright and sociable.

Organization is the key to success. Rush around before the guests arrive, but on no account when they are there. I like to serve champagne to start, although I'm not impartial to a vodka and tonic with lime.

It's a happy thing indeed to watch the evening open out, like a Chinese paper flower in a bowl of water. Best of all I like to have someone perched on one of the bar stools, talking to me while I'm cooking — it's like putting music to ballet.

After this beginning, I take myself off and do the main course. By now, I have to tear myself away. But it has its compensations. I have the pleasure of hearing everyone talking not so far away. The main course is served; it may take a while, but it doesn't matter. Eaten with relish, it's often followed by one good cheese and then fruit. But sometimes I indulge, and make the sweetest of sweets.

With the fish course, I'd serve Sancerre or a Muscadet de Sèvre et Maine sur lie (the last two words are important — it's much finer), and nothing with the dessert. The usual after-dinner drinks are conducive to conversation, but heavy — back to the champagne? Coffee follows, then a chance to sit back and reflect, mellow as marshmallows.

There comes a time when the imaginary party hats, and the streamers which seemed to be pulled all over the place when someone told that silly old joke, have disappeared; serious subjects have been dived into and out of again. Taxis are hailed, coats put on and lifts called for. As each purring black cab fades into the distant, dark night, I hope the smiles won't.

TEMPURA VEGETABLES WITH DIPPING SAUCE

This appeals to my love of very crunchy batter.

SERVES 6

oil for deep frying

3 large carrots, cut lengthways into 5mm/¼in strips, then again into 5cm/2in lengths

3 large celery stalks, halved lengthways and cut into 5cm/2in lengths

2 onions, sliced into 5mm/¼in thick circles and opened out into rings

75g/3oz mange-touts

FOR THE BATTER

2 large eggs

200ml/7fl. oz very cold water with an ice cube floating in it

¼ teaspoon bicarbonate of soda

75g/3oz plain flour

25g/1oz cornflour

FOR THE SAUCE

50ml/2fl. oz soy sauce, preferably Japanese

50ml/2fl. oz sake or dry sherry

1. Heat the oil in a wok or deep-fat fryer to 375F/190C.

2. Put the eggs into a bowl with the water and ice cube, and beat until frothy. When ready to mix the batter, add the bicarbonate of soda to the eggs.

3. Add the flours, unsifted, and mix together with chopsticks. Do this briefly (you can use two forks instead of chopsticks) — you want lumps of flour in the mixture. Use the batter straight away if you can, although it will hold its volume for up to 5 minutes.

4. When the oil is hot enough, dip the vegetables, a few pieces at a time, into the batter. Fry the carrots and celery for about 2 minutes, flipping the pieces over halfway through. The batter should literally explode and puff up.

5. Drain on absorbent paper. Eat at once if possible, otherwise keep hot in an oven heated to 220C/425F/gas 7 for no longer than 5 minutes. Dip the onion rings and mange-touts in the batter; fry in the same way for 1 minute.

6. Serve in little piles with the dipping sauce, simply made by mixing the soy sauce and sake lightly together.

COUNTDOWN

The day before
• *Make the fish stock and leave to cool. Chill it, unstrained, in the refrigerator.*

On the day
• *Strain the stock and reduce it.*
• *Meanwhile, open the oysters or can of clams: add the juice to the reducing stock. Chill the oysters or clams.*
• *Prepare the fruits for dessert. Make the caramel, dip the fruits. Leave to set.*
• *Prepare the vegetables for the tempura.*
• *Measure out the flours. Beat the egg with the iced water and chill.*
• *Prepare the fish. Chop the leeks.*

Half an hour before serving
• *Prepare the salad dressing.*

Just before serving
• *Heat the oil for the tempura.*
• *Mix the batter; add the soda.*
• *Fry the vegetables.*

After the first course
• *Make the sauce and keep warm in a bowl over hot water.*
• *Cook the fish and leeks with the oysters or clams. Toss salad with dressing.*

HAKE WITH OYSTER SABAYON

This main course illustrates my fascination with reducing stock for sauce. The intensity of flavour is just astounding.

SERVES 6

18 oysters or 425g/15oz clams canned in natural juice
6 hake steaks, skinned and trimmed of any outside bone, about 2cm/¾in thick
2 tablespoons safflower oil
50g/2oz butter
250g/8oz leeks, trimmed weight, white and a bit of green, cut into 7.5cm/3in lengths and shredded lengthways
sprigs of coriander to garnish
FOR THE STOCK
1 carrot
1 onion
1 celery stalk
fish heads, bones and skin
few sprigs of fresh fennel leaf, parsley and thyme
few black peppercorns
crushed salt
6 tablespoons white wine or champagne vinegar
FOR THE SAUCE
2 egg yolks
1 tablespoon double cream
4 tablespoons hot reduced fish stock (see recipe)
100g/4oz cold unsalted butter, diced
few squeezes of lemon juice
salt and white pepper

1. First, make the fish stock. Chop the vegetables coarsely, then put all the ingredients into a pan with about 1L/2pts water and bring to the boil. Skim off any scum, then simmer for 20 minutes. (You can do this the day before and leave it unstrained in the refrigerator overnight.)

2. Leave to cool, then strain. Reduce the stock by fast boiling to about 4 tablespoons: this will take about 1 hour, although you should check after 35-40 minutes, as the size, shape and thickness of the pan, and the cooker heat, can all affect the timing.

3. Meanwhile, if you are using the oysters, open them over a bowl and add the liquor to the reducing stock. If using clams, drain and add the can liquor. Keep oysters or clams in a covered container in the refrigerator.

4. Prepare a pan of gently simmering water. Put the egg yolks and cream into a bowl which will fit over the saucepan. The water must not touch the base of the bowl, otherwise the eggs will cook and harden.

5. Whisk the egg yolks and cream over the water until frothy and thickened. Gradually whisk in the hot reduced stock, a tablespoon at a time.

6. Add the chilled butter, a piece at a time, whisking until it has melted and has been absorbed by the sauce before adding the next piece. Add a squeeze of lemon juice and season to taste. Turn off the heat and leave the sauce over the warm water, whisking now and again to stop a skin forming. It will last like this for 10-15 minutes, while you cook the fish.

7. Heat the grill to moderately high. Brush the fish steaks with the oil and grill for 3 minutes each side, brushing the other side when you turn the steaks.

8. Meanwhile, melt the butter and fry the leeks for about 3 minutes — you want them softened but still with a bit of bite.

9. Add the oysters or clams to the leeks for the last minute to heat through. You may not need to use all the clams.

10. Arrange the fish steaks on warmed serving plates, top with the leeks and oysters or clams, and a few spoonfuls of the sauce.

11. Garnish with sprigs of coriander, and serve with the remaining sauce, accompanied by a dressed crisp, green salad.

WINE NOTES

*Though the relatively
inexpensive supermarket own-
brand champagnes are
admirably suited to informal
kitchen and supper parties,
they do vary rather a lot in
quality and style. It pays to
buy what you require six to
nine months in advance, and to
lay the bottles down in a dark,
undisturbed corner where the
temperature is stable. The
extra bottle age will round out
and much improve flavour and
quality.*

*I must say I am seldom
excited by Muscadet, but it's a
pleasant, bland, rather neutral
quaffing wine most of the time.
An increasing number of
Muscadets do have an
interesting flavour and some
real structure and weight,
particularly those from
Chéreau-Carré, which are full,
fruity and fresh.*

*For Sancerre, recommended
producers include Lucien
Crochet, Vincent Delaporte,
Bernard and Jean Reverdy,
Pierre and Etienne Riffault,
and Jean Vatan. The wines are
pungent and curranty. A wine
made from the same
Sauvignon grape in a
weightier, more profound style
is Cloudy Bay Sauvignon from
New Zealand, where David
Hohnen has discovered a new
dimension in Sauvignon's
potential.*

*Although Coralie Dorman
finds after-dinner wines heavy,
Clos St Georges Graves
Supérieur is still a honeyed
snip that would go a treat with
lightly carmelized fruits, and
Cuvée José Sala Muscat is
considerably lighter and
cheaper than Muscat de
Beaumes de Venise.*

FRUIT IN CARAMEL COATS

Fruit wrapped in a glass case of sugar delights eyes and mouths. Bite through the case and the fruit, as perfect as ever, explodes its juices. Make these only a few hours before the meal as the caramel tends to soften.

SERVES 6

a selection of fresh fruit: cherries, strawberries, lychees, kumquats, black and green grapes

FOR THE CARAMEL

500g/1lb granulated sugar

good pinch of cream of tartar

1. First, prepare the fruits. Use any firm fruits but not those that leak juices. They must be undamaged and absolutely dry before dipping into the caramel. Don't stone the cherries but hull the strawberries. Peel the lychees and stone if liked. Leave kumquats whole. If liked, remove the pips from the grapes with a large needle — or use seedless grapes.

2. Put the sugar and enough water to cover into a pan. Aim to use about one-third the amount of water to sugar, in this case about 175ml/6fl. oz water.

3. Dissolve the sugar in the water slowly, without stirring. Dissolve the cream of tartar in 2 teaspoons water; add to the syrup as soon as the sugar dissolves. Bring to the boil, then boil steadily until the syrup reaches 150C/300F on a sugar thermometer, or until the liquid thickens slightly and turns a pale gold colour — about 15 minutes. Remove from the heat and plunge the base of the pan into cold water to prevent further cooking. Dip in the fruit pieces, one at a time. Use a long-handled fork for this. Place on very lightly greased greaseproof paper and leave to set.

Fay Maschler

SUNDAY LUNCH

Celebrate the weekend with a splendid family lunch. Fay Maschler's unusual menu makes Sunday the highlight of the week

---

Crab mayonnaise on shrimp crackers
Prawns piri-piri
Fried cashew nuts

Bollito misto
Red and green sauces
Crisply cooked cabbage
White haricot beans

Salad Italian style
Cheese

Surprising lemon pudding
Nuts, fruit and chocolates

Sunday lunch is a meal that myths surround. It is symbolic of family unity, synonymous with indulgence and lethargy, and stuck forever with the image of roast beef.

I like Sunday lunch for obliging me to shop on Saturday. Journalism and its deadlines invariably result in the character defect of leaving everything to the last minute, which in my case also includes the preparation of food.

What I like to cook is governed to some extent by what I have been eating during the previous week. I incline towards boiled or poached food, on which few restaurants capitalise.

I maintain that boiled meat has a truer flavour. It is healthier, less fattening and provides an ideal vehicle for interesting sauces and garnishes. I love boiled leg of lamb with caper sauce, and *boeuf à la ficelle*, where you dangle the parcel of meat on a string in boiling water. But best of all possible worlds is the Italian dish of mixed boiled meats, *bollito misto*. It is a traditional Sunday lunch dish in Italian restaurants, especially those of Lombardy and Piedmont, but can work admirably at home when you have a number of people to entertain.

The choice of meats should be dictated by personal preference but it is essential, in my view, to have a salted cut such as gammon or tongue, a white meat such as chicken or guinea fowl, some beef or veal and a very superior sausage — *cotechino* or *zampone*, available from Italian grocers, are best, but any noble boiling sausage will suffice. The assembly of meats results in the best leftover of all: a wonderful stock for future soups. Any meat remaining is ideal for an interesting meat salad the following day, with green sauce as a dressing.

A selection of sauces is one of the keys to a successful *bollito misto*. I like to enliven the tomato-based

COUNTDOWN

The day before
- *Prepare the red and green sauces.*
- *Mix together the crab mayonnaise.*
- *Set the haricot beans to soak.*

In the morning
- *About $3\frac{3}{4}$ hours ahead start the bollito misto. Put the tongue and trotter in boiling water. After 30 minutes add the beef. After 1 hour add the chicken; simmer 1 hour and stand 45 minutes. Skin the tongue and put the sausage to simmer separately.*
  Meanwhile:
- *Prepare the salad leaves.*
- *Prepare the pudding, leaving only the whites of eggs to be beaten and folded in just before you put it in the oven.*
- *Wash and chop the cabbage and leave in a plastic bag in the refrigerator.*
- *Assemble your cheeses.*
- *Lastly, start boiling the haricot beans.*

When the guests arrive or just before
- *Spread the crab mixture on the shrimp crackers.*
- *Fry the cashew nuts.*
- *Fry the prawns.*

Just before sitting down
- *Put the cabbage on to boil.*

While your helper carves
- *Toss the drained tender cabbage in butter.*
- *Drain the haricot beans, and season and gloss with a choice of fat.*
- *Whisk egg whites, fold into pudding mixture and set in the oven.*

After the main course
- *Dress the salad.*

sauce with the bite of chilli. I also serve a bowl of chopped *mostarda di frutta*: a mixture of fruits in a sweet and sour sauce flavoured with mustard and garlic, which you can buy at Italian shops. Dried white haricot beans, soaked and boiled, are a typical accompaniment. I also make a dish of pasta. Crisply cooked cabbage is the chosen vegetable.

Such a substantial main course is only eroded in its impact by a first course, so my ploy is to serve a few items with drinks beforehand. After the main course and before the dessert I would offer at the most two Italian cheeses, and perhaps only one, with a green salad dressed Italian-style with lemon juice or Balsamic vinegar and olive oil. The lemon pudding is a nursery dessert that appeals to adults and children alike. Although it has a spongy topping, it is light and sings with a citrus flavour. It can be prepared in advance up to step 2.

And since Sunday lunch should take over the day, serve fruit, nuts and chocolate with tea or coffee.

CRAB MAYONNAISE ON SHRIMP CRACKERS

These little snacks are ideal with pre-lunch cocktails (preferably champagne); they are simple to prepare at the last minute and they aren't too filling.

SERVES 8
100-175g/4-6oz frozen crab meat, defrosted
2 tablespoons good-quality mayonnaise
2 teaspoons lemon juice
dash of Tabasco
freshly ground black pepper
1 packet cooked Chinese shrimp crackers

1. Mix the well-drained crab meat with mayonnaise and lemon juice. Season with a dash of Tabasco and freshly ground black pepper. Place a spoonful on each shrimp cracker.

PRAWNS PIRI-PIRI

Serve these delicious bites instead of a starter. Add more or less chilli powder, depending on how hot you like them.

SERVES 8
3 tablespoons vegetable oil
2 garlic cloves, peeled and roughly chopped
$\frac{1}{4}$-1 teaspoon chilli powder (depending on taste)
700g/1$\frac{1}{2}$lb small brown shrimps or 350g/12oz shelled prawns

1. Heat the vegetable oil, preferably in a small earthenware flameproof dish. When the oil is sizzling add the garlic and chilli powder. Stir round and add the shrimps or prawns to the flameproof dish.

2. Stir quickly with a wooden fork or spoon until they are hot. Serve the shrimps or prawns immediately with toothpicks for spearing them.

Clockwise from left: crab mayonnaise on shrimp crackers; prawns piri-piri; fried cashew nuts

BOLLITO MISTO

One large pan into which you can fit all the meat is the ideal, but if necessary you can use two. Simmer the boiling sausage separately, or it will spoil the stock.

SERVES 8
2 carrots
2 celery stalks
1 onion
1 small salted ox tongue or 700g/1½lb gammon
2 pig's trotters or 1 calf's foot, split (optional)
1kg/2lb boiling beef such as brisket, silverside or topside, tied in a piece, or 1kg/2lb shoulder of veal, boned and tied in a piece
1 boiling or roasting chicken
1 boiling sausage

1. Choose a pan large enough to take all the vegetables and meat with enough water to cover. Put the vegetables in the pan with the water and bring to the boil. The water must be boiling to seal in the meat juices.
2. Add the tongue, and the trotters or calf's foot, if using, and bring water to a simmer, cover and cook for 30 minutes. Add the beef and continue to simmer for a further 30 minutes, skimming off scum from the surface. Now add the chicken, if it is a boiling fowl. Add the boned veal shoulder, if it is to be used instead of beef.
3. After simmering for another 30 minutes, add the gammon joint if included instead of the tongue, and the chicken if it is a roaster. Simmer for 1 hour, then turn off the heat; leave for 45 minutes. Using the tongue, the *bollito misto* will take 3 hours to cook plus standing time, but if the gammon and veal are used it will take 2 hours plus standing time.
4. After the tongue has been simmered for 3 hours, remove it from the pot and skin it; make a slit on the top side and it should peel away quite easily. Trim off any fat or gristle before returning the tongue to the pot. Bring the stock back to the boil; cover the pan and turn off the heat. Start simmering the sausage in water in a separate pan.
5. Warm a large flat serving dish. Carve about two-thirds of the meat and sausage. Arrange the slices on the dish and moisten with several spoonfuls of stock before serving.

RED SAUCE
(*SALSA ROSSA*)

SERVES 8
½ fresh green chilli pepper
1 fat garlic clove
sea salt
4 large ripe tomatoes, blanched, peeled, seeded and finely chopped
1 tablespoon olive oil
2 teaspoons red wine vinegar
4 spring onions, finely chopped
1 teaspoon lemon or lime juice
good pinch of dried oregano
black pepper

1. Trim away the stalk and the inner membranes from the chilli; discard the seeds. Chop the chilli extremely finely. Crush the garlic clove with a little sea salt and mix in with the chilli. Stir this into the chopped tomatoes and then add the oil, vinegar, onions, lemon juice and oregano.
2. Allow the flavours to mingle for at least an hour or so and season with salt and freshly ground pepper just before serving. The red sauce can also be prepared the day before serving to obtain the most from the flavours.

Overleaf: bollito misto with red and green sauces, cabbage and haricot beans

FRIED CASHEW NUTS

Cashew nuts fried at home have a completely different taste from the familiar, heavily-salted, bought roasted nuts. Raw cashew nuts are widely available these days in wholefood and health food shops, Chinese and Asian grocers and many of the larger conventional supermarkets.

SERVES 8
vegetable oil for frying
250g/8oz raw cashew nuts
salt and black pepper

1. Heat about 2.5cm/1in of oil in a deep frying pan or sauté pan. Add the nuts and fry them until lightly coloured. Empty them into a sieve and shake off the oil. Spread them on kitchen paper once and then again to remove all traces of grease. Sprinkle with salt and freshly ground black pepper, and serve the nuts warm.

GREEN SAUCE
(SALSA VERDE)

SERVES 8

6 anchovy fillets, mashed

4 tablespoons finely chopped parsley

2 tablespoons finely chopped capers

1 garlic clove, peeled and finely chopped

1 teaspoon Dijon mustard

1 teaspoon red wine vinegar, plus extra

8 tablespoons olive oil

black pepper

1 soft-boiled egg (optional)

1. Put the anchovy fillets into a bowl, mash with a fork, then pound with a wooden spoon, as you stir in the parsley, capers, garlic, mustard and then the vinegar. Add the olive oil slowly, beating it in as when making mayonnaise. Season with freshly ground pepper and, if you think it requires it, more vinegar. If you like the idea of the egg, stir in the yolk just before serving and add the egg white finely chopped.

CRISPLY COOKED
CABBAGE

SERVES 8

1 Dutch white or firm Savoy cabbage

75g/3oz butter

salt and black pepper

pinch of grated nutmeg

2 teaspoons caraway seeds (optional)

1. Peel off any discoloured outer leaves from the cabbage and cut away the heftier parts of the stalk. Cut into fairly thick slices. Bring a large quantity of salted water to the boil and tip in all the cabbage. Cook briskly for about 5 minutes until the cabbage is just tender.
2. Drain well. Sauté the cabbage in the butter, seasoning with salt and freshly ground pepper, nutmeg and the caraway seeds. Contrary to the popular opinion about boiling vegetables in hardly any water, I think cabbage, anyway, retains its essence far better by being boiled in copious quantities.

SALAD ITALIAN STYLE

SERVES 8

a mixture of at least three leaves: radicchio, curly endive, lamb's lettuce, oak leaf lettuce, watercress, baby spinach leaves, etc.

4 tablespoons extra virgin olive oil

sea salt and black pepper

1 tablespoon lemon juice or Balsamic vinegar

1. Wash the salad leaves if necessary, drying with kitchen paper, tearing into small pieces and keeping for a few hours in a plastic bag in the refrigerator.
2. Just before serving, tip the leaves into a large salad bowl. Add the oil and toss. Sprinkle with salt and freshly ground pepper and toss again, so that the leaves are well coated. Sprinkle on the lemon or vinegar and toss again.

WHITE HARICOT BEANS

Beans from Soissons are nicest if you can find them. Don't keep haricot beans, though, longer than a year: they will remain bullet hard however long you cook them.

SERVES 8

500g/1lb white dried haricot beans, soaked overnight

1 large onion, stuck with a clove

1 large carrot, cut into chunks

50g/2oz butter or chicken, duck or goose fat

salt and black pepper

2 tablespoons chopped fresh parsley

1. If you haven't soaked the beans boil them in plenty of water for 5 minutes; turn off the heat and leave for 1 hour. Drain the beans and cover them with cold water. Add the onion and carrot and boil for about 1 hour until the beans are tender but not mushy, then drain and remove onion and clove.
2. Turn into a serving dish, add the fat and let it melt in. Add salt and pepper and stir carefully. Sprinkle with chopped parsley just before serving.

SURPRISING LEMON
PUDDING

The surprise is the two-tone effect: a spongy top with a golden creamy lemon sauce below. Serve with a sweetened raspberry or currant purée, if liked.

SERVES 8

100g/4oz butter

grated zest and juice of 2 small lemons

200g/7oz caster sugar

4 eggs, separated

50g/2oz plain flour

about 450ml/¾pt creamy milk

pinch of salt

1. Heat the oven to 180C/350F/gas 4. Cream the butter with the grated lemon zest and the sugar. Beat the egg yolks into the creamed butter. Add the sifted flour alternately with lemon juice made up to 600ml/1pt with the milk (this will curdle).
2. Whisk the egg whites with a pinch of salt until they form stiff peaks. Fold into the lemony mixture. Pour into a large soufflé dish and bake for about 45 minutes.

Above: salad Italian style and cheese.
Right: surprising lemon pudding (top); nuts, fruit and chocolates (bottom)

WINE NOTES

Fay Maschler says that before this meal she would serve champagne cocktails – made with a lump of sugar, a dash of brandy and a teaspoon of Seville orange juice, garnished with a slice of Seville orange. Champagne could be a supermarket brand, or a méthode champenoise *from some other region of production.*

Extravagant as it may sound, champagne as an aperitif can often be more economical than fiddling about with a costly variety of different drinks.

To accompany bollito misto *a dry Lambrusco would be a good choice, but if you have any reservations about a pétillant red wine, a Barbera, less heavy than a Barolo, makes an acceptable alternative.*

Asti Spumante is under-appreciated and often delicious. It accompanies sweet food like the pudding very well, otherwise you might like a Moscato or a Recioto di Soave.

33

Lisa Kinsman

CHINESE SEAFOOD DINNER

As refreshing as a breath of sea air, Lisa Kinsman's menu is a foretaste of summer's delights

---

Fresh crab and coriander crispy bundles
Stuffed mussels with mixed seafood
Seaweed

Stir-fried monkfish with green peppers and soya beans
Stir-fried squid and vegetables
Fried rice with oyster sauce

Fruit extravaganza
Floating islands

Chinese food is designed for sharing and is ideal for parties. It stimulates conversation, and the numerous dishes that make up a meal ensure that interest, both visually and in taste, is maintained throughout.

When invited to my house for a dinner party, my friends expect the food to be Chinese. But serving one dish at a time in the traditional Chinese way means I have to spend the entire evening in the kitchen and have just enough time to say a brief hello and goodbye to my friends, so I serve the food in three courses as Europeans do.

All the starter dishes can be prepared in advance, needing only a little last-minute attention. They are usually finger foods, and I like to serve them on plates rather than in bowls, which is the traditional method, as they look much more appealing this way.

The ground fried fish used for topping the seaweed is especially pretty, being a salmon-pink powder made from sea bass, salt, flour, sugar, soya beans and safflower oil. It has an unusual smoky flavour.

I have chosen two light and colourful stir-fry dishes for the main course, because most of the preparation and cooking can be done well in advance.

To accompany these two dishes, I have selected fried rice with oyster sauce. This rice dish can also be cooked well in advance, and can be reheated in a microwave oven or, wrapped in foil with a couple of slits on the top, in a conventional oven.

The stir-fry dishes can be cooked in two stages. The first stage, which

COUNTDOWN

The day before
• *Fry the flaked almonds (if using) and shred the spinach or spring greens for the seaweed.*
• *Prepare and cook the crab and coriander filling for the crispy bundles.*
• *Prepare and cook the stuffing for the stuffed mussels.*
• *Trim and cut up the monkfish and the squid.*

In the morning
• *Make the floating islands, but do not add the caramel yet.*
• *Stuff the mussels and chill them.*

In the afternoon
• *Boil the rice.*
• *Make the bundles.*
• *Fry the stuffed mussels.*
• *Slice the radish and green pepper for the stir-fried squid and monkfish.*

Two hours before the meal
• *Fry the rice, the crispy bundles and the spinach or spring greens.*

30 minutes before guests arrive
• *Run the monkfish and then the squid through the oil.*
• *Prepare the fruit tray.*

15-20 minutes before serving
• *Reheat the mussels, rice and the crispy bundles in the oven.*
• *Lay a bed of seaweed, mustard and cress or washed leaves on the platter for the mussels.*
• *Garnish the seaweed.*

After the first course
• *Finish cooking the stir-fried monkfish and squid dishes.*

After the main course
• *Prepare the caramel.*

can be done in advance, is a brief deep fry involving 30 seconds' cooking at a high temperature. This is to seal the ingredient and prevent it from breaking up; it gives a clean, neat finish to the dish, with no seeping juice to spoil its appearance. This method, called 'running through the oil', helps to reduce the time needed for stir-frying a dish, and so it is very useful when cooking for a dinner party.

I find that dessert is as important as the starter and main courses. It is always a treat to see a choice of puddings on a sweet trolley in a restaurant. Obviously we cannot indulge too much at a private party, but two kinds of dessert give an option.

Maybe this is the Chinese in me: I always say 'two are better than one', since we always have more than one dish to each course.

Fresh fruit is one of my passions, but a simple bowl of mixed fruit does not seem to do it justice, especially now that exotic fruits are available all year round. I would choose a selection of fruit: strawberries, cherries, pomegranates, physalis, and grapes laid out on a platter. Each fruit has its own beauty of form, texture, colour and flavour, and can be coated in a layer of caramel as an 'extravaganza'.

The dish floating islands is one of my specialities; it brings back memories of my childhood. When I first tasted it in a European restaurant in Hong Kong at the age of 10, it was just plain floating islands. But later, I had the idea of enclosing it with a golden cloud of spun sugar to make it a bit more glamorous. The same caramel mixture can be used to coat the fruit for the extravaganza, if liked.

Although the Chinese do not usually drink wine with their meal, they do drink tea and spirits such as whisky and brandy. However, I find that a number of European wines complement Chinese food. I myself prefer to drink wines from the Sauvignon grape, such as Sancerre and Pouilly Fumé from the Loire Valley. Other crisp, dry wines like Chardonnay or Chablis are very good and complement the food perfectly. Alsatian wines with their spicy fragrant taste also go very well with Chinese dishes.

If red wines are preferred, any of the Beaujolais are excellent, as is a light, fresh and delicate Italian red wine such as Valpolicella or Bardolino.

Finally, any good chilled rosé wine may be chosen as a happy accompaniment, and its colour may well be a further recommendation.

FRESH CRAB AND CORIANDER CRISPY BUNDLES

A variation on the popular chicken and beansprout spring roll.

SERVES 8
corn oil for deep frying
100g/4oz Spanish onion, finely sliced
salt and pepper
100g/4oz white crab meat
1 teaspoon cornflower mixed with ½ tablespoon water
½-1 teaspoon curry power
½ teaspoon sugar
25g/1oz fresh coriander, chopped
spring-roll paper

1. In a hot wok, heat ½ tablespoon oil to a medium temperature and stir-fry the onion with a pinch of salt until softened; transfer the onion to a dish.
2. Heat another tablespoon oil to a high temperature and add the crab meat; stir-fry for 1 minute. Then add the fried onion, cornflour mixture, curry powder, sugar and the coriander. Stir well, taste, and season. Transfer to a dish, cover and chill in the refrigerator.
3. Cut the spring-roll paper into eight 7.5cm/3in squares and eight 20 × 1cm/ 8 × ½in strips. Place 1 teaspoon of the filling in the centre of each square and

gather the corners of the paper to form a bundle. Knot a long strip around the bundle, taking care not to break it. Make the remaining bundles in the same way (any leftover filling can be made into small rolls). Transfer to a tray, cover with cling film and chill in the refrigerator for several hours or overnight. Pull out the tops of the bundles to resemble petals.

4. In a wok heat about 600ml/1pt oil to a moderate temperature and fry the bundles, 2 at a time, for 1-2 minutes, until they are golden. Drain them on kitchen paper and place the bundles on a wire rack. Serve at once or reheat them in the oven if you have made them in advance.

Note:

Spring-roll paper is paper-thin white pastry which comes in sheets about 20cm/8in square. It is available from Chinese supermarkets and may be stored, well wrapped, in the freezer.

STUFFED MUSSELS WITH MIXED SEAFOOD

This is a dish that can be prepared and cooked in advance, and reheated just before serving.

SERVES 8

1kg/2lb mussels, scrubbed and bearded

5 scallops

salt and pepper

3 tablespoons corn oil

100g/4oz Spanish onion, finely chopped

100g/4oz cooked, peeled prawns, halved (defrosted and dried on kitchen paper if frozen)

25g/1oz spring onions, finely chopped

½ teaspoon sugar

1 tablespoon cornflour mixed with 3 tablespoons water

50g/2oz dry white breadcrumbs

seaweed, mustard and cress or washed leaves to garnish

1. In a covered pan, cook the mussels over a high heat until opened. Discard any that remain closed. Remove the shells and chop the flesh roughly. Clean the interiors of the mussel shells with a sharp knife.

2. Separate the scallop corals from the white flesh and dry well with kitchen paper; season the roes. Heat 2 teaspoons of the oil and fry the scallop roes over a low heat until lightly browned on both sides. Remove them from the pan. Turn up the heat and fry the white flesh in the same way, then chop the roes and flesh.

3. Heat 2 teaspoons of oil to a medium temperature and stir-fry the Spanish onion with a pinch of salt for 1 minute; remove to a bowl.

4. Heat 2 teaspoons of the oil and stir-fry the mussels and prawns briefly before adding the onion, scallops, spring onions, sugar and cornflour mixture. Continue to stir-fry until the mixture thickens, then season with salt and pepper to taste.

5. Fill the mussel shells with the seafood mixture and sprinkle the breadcrumbs on top. Press down gently to make a neat shape. Chill the stuffed mussels for a few hours. Then brown them in a shallow pan, a few at a time, with just a couple of drops of oil. Place the stuffed mussels on a baking tray to be reheated later. (The stuffed mussels may be browned under the grill, if you prefer.)

6. Serve hot, garnished with seaweed, mustard and cress or garden leaves.

SEAWEED

SERVES 8

25g/1oz ground fried fish, or 50g/2oz flaked almonds

700g/1½lb fresh spinach, or 1kg/2lb spring greens

600ml/1pt oil

salt and pepper

caster sugar for sprinkling

1. Fry the flaked almonds (if using) in a shallow pan without any oil until they become golden, then spread them out on kitchen paper.

2. Wash the leaves of the spinach or spring greens and remove the central fibres, drying the leaves thoroughly to remove all traces of moisture. Roll several leaves tightly together, almost like a cigar, and cut the roll lengthways into strips about 3mm/⅛in thick; separate the strands.

3. Heat the oil to 120C/250F in a wok. Turn off the heat before adding the spinach to the oil, a good handful at a time. (Care must be taken as the oil could splatter a little.) Turn on the heat again and deep fry the spinach for about 3 minutes or until it turns a darker green in colour.

4. Remove the spinach with a large slotted spoon and rest it in a wire sieve, before draining in a baking tray lined with kitchen paper. The spinach will become crisp as it cooks. Season the spinach with salt, pepper and a little sugar. (The seaweed may be stored in an airtight tin.)

5. Before serving, turn three-quarters of the seaweed into a warm serving dish and sprinkle the ground fried fish or fried almond flakes on top; reserve the rest to garnish the stuffed mussels (see previous recipe).

STIR-FRIED MONKFISH WITH GREEN PEPPERS AND SOYA BEANS

SERVES 8

1.5kg/3¼lb monkfish, skinned and filleted
1 teaspoon cornflour
salt and pepper
300ml/½pt corn oil
1 tablespoon canned black soya beans, finely chopped
1 large green pepper, halved, seeded, and finely sliced
1 tablespoon shaoshing wine or medium dry sherry
½ teaspoon sugar

1. Cut the fish into 4 × 1cm/2 × ½in pieces and put them in a bowl with the cornflour, salt and pepper. Heat the oil in a wok to a high temperature, run the

fish through the oil (see page 36) for about 30 seconds, then drain the pieces in a wire sieve.

2. Just before serving, heat 2 teaspoons of oil to a high temperature, stir-fry the soya beans briefly and then add the fish. Stir-fry for about 2 minutes, then add the green pepper, shaoshing wine and sugar, and continue to stir-fry for 1 minute. Serve in a warmed dish.

Note:

Black soya beans – fermented and with a strong salty taste – are available dried or canned from Chinese grocers.

STIR-FRIED SQUID AND VEGETABLES

SERVES 8

1.1kg/2½lb baby squid, cleaned
salt and pepper
300ml/½pt corn oil for frying
4-6 thin slices fresh root ginger
2 garlic cloves, crushed
350g/12oz fresh beansprouts
2 tablespoons sweet and chilli sauce (available from Chinese stores)
2 tablespoons light soy sauce
2 tablespoons tomato ketchup
175g/6oz radish, thinly sliced

1. Cut the squid tentacles into short lengths. Cut the bodies open lengthways, lay them flat on a board and lightly score their surfaces in a crisscross pattern. Cut them into small pieces of roughly equal size and place them in a bowl. Sprinkle with salt and pepper.

2. In a wok, heat the oil. Run the squid quickly through the oil in 2 batches, remove from the oil and drain.

3. Heat a tablespoon of oil to a very high temperature and stir-fry the ginger and garlic for 20-30 seconds, pressing them down to extract as much of their juice as possible. Discard the garlic and ginger and heat the oil until it smokes, and then add the beansprouts with a light sprinkling of salt. Stir-fry for 1 minute, and then drain the beansprouts in a wire sieve.

4. Heat another tablespoon of oil to a

Clockwise from left: fried rice with oyster sauce; stir-fried squid and vegetables; and stir-fried monkfish with green peppers and soya beans

very high temperature, stir-fry the squid, sweet and chilli sauce, soy sauce and tomato ketchup for about 3 minutes, then add the beansprouts and the radish. Continue to stir-fry for another 1-2 minutes, then transfer to a heated serving dish.

FRIED RICE WITH OYSTER SAUCE

SERVES 8

3 tablespoons corn oil
350g/12oz carrots, finely chopped
250g/8oz French beans, finely chopped
salt
350g/12oz long-grain rice, cooked
3 tablespoons oyster sauce
pepper

1. Heat half the oil to a high temperature, stir-fry the carrots and the French beans with a pinch of salt for about a minute, then transfer the vegetables to a bowl.

2. In the same pan, heat the remaining oil to a high temperature. Stir-fry the rice for 1 minute, then add the oyster sauce, and the vegetables; stir well for 2 minutes, then season with pepper and transfer the rice and vegetables to a serving dish.

WINE NOTES

As Lisa Kinsman suggests, a wide variety of wines might happily accompany this meal, and it is certainly not difficult to enjoy wine with Chinese food like this. I confess that my own preference, when eating Chinese food in restaurants, is to order Alsace wine – either the soft and distinctively scented Gewürztraminer or the firm, full and slightly spicy Pinot Blanc – because they are usually of highly dependable quality and still relatively cheap.

Wines from the local co-operatives in Alsace, or merchants like Trimbach, Hugel and Kuentz-Bas, or growers like Mure of Rouffach, are all unlikely to disappoint.

Though squid and monkfish are both particularly meaty forms of seafood, with which red wine or Chardonnay might go very pleasingly, my own inclination with both the crab spring rolls and the stir-fried food would be to go for the crisper style and sharper texture of fresh and fruity Sauvignon. It need not be a pricey classic: modern wineries are turning out better and better examples at modest prices from lesser regions too.

Italian light red wines are rather risky. Ensure, if you can, that the stock is really fresh. An occasionally fine alternative to those, or to the more familiar Beaujolais, is Pinot Noir d'Alsace, a red so light that it is almost rosé. Turckheim co-operative is particularly good at it, just as the producers of the Presque-Ile de St Tropez make the ▶

Wine Notes (continued)

finest pink Côtes de Provence you are likely to find.

For a dessert wine I think your guests would be suitably impressed with a little Australian Noble Late Harvested Botrytis Sémillon – down under's firm and assertive response to Sauternes.

Floating islands and fruit extravaganza

FLOATING ISLANDS

SERVES 8

1L/2pt milk
8 size 2 eggs, separated
50g/2oz caster sugar
150ml/¼pt single cream
½-1 teaspoon vanilla essence
FOR THE CARAMEL
250g/8oz caster sugar
pinch of cream of tartar

1. Heat the milk in a wok on a medium-high temperature. Turn down the heat to low as the milk begins to boil.

2. Whisk the egg whites with an electric whisk until stiff. Lower rounded dessertspoons of white into the milk and poach them for about 2 minutes on both sides. Carefully lift them out of the milk with a large slotted spoon and drain them on layers of kitchen paper. Allow the milk to cool slightly, then beat the yolks and the sugar until creamy, and mix with the warm milk.

3. Strain the mixture through a wire sieve into a clean pan. Heat the mixture gently, stirring constantly with a wooden spoon until it thickens. Add the cream and the vanilla essence, before pouring into a serving dish, again through a wire sieve. (I find the custard is always perfect even without using a double-boiler.)

4. Gently place the poached egg whites (the best side up) on top of the custard and chill, uncovered.

5. To make the caramel, boil 350ml/12fl.oz water with the sugar and the cream of tartar in a small heavy-based pan until the liquid thickens slightly and begins to turn a light gold — it will take about 15 minutes. Swirl the pan to even the colour. Watch it carefully, taking care not to let it burn. Remove the pan from the heat. (Now is the best time to coat the fruit for the extravaganza.)

6. Let the caramel stand for 5 minutes, then dip a pair of chopsticks into it and lift them to head height over the bowl of floating islands. The caramel will fall thread-like over the meringues. Ease the sugar strands from the chopsticks with your fingers to form a cloud-like shape Serve with a selection of fruit.

Antonio Carluccio

ITALIAN FLAIR

As summer approaches and the evenings lengthen, lighter meals are the order of the day. But they need not be boring, as Antonio Carluccio's appetizing menu demonstrates

---

Scallops in their shells with coriander and ginger sauce

Ricotta and spinach pockets

Jacket chicken breasts

Terrine of sorbets with raspberry sauce

In the West, impressive and healthy are not generally thought of as words that live happily together when food is the subject. But cuisines from all over the world show us that healthy ingredients can be used to create sensational dishes. Too often in this country healthy food is boring to eat and to look at, so I have taken care to plan recipes that appeal to the eye as well as to the palate. I hope that you enjoy making them and that your dinner party is a delightful success.

Two big scallops per person are sufficient to start an elegant dinner. The first recipe, which slightly resembles some Chinese specialities, is simple to prepare. The freshness of the scallops is essential. Your fishmonger should be prepared to open and clean the shells for you. Take the scallops home attached to the flat shells, and take the curved ones to serve them in.

Home-made pasta pockets filled with low-fat ricotta cheese are extremely healthy, but also special enough to please even the most discriminating of guests. As a second course you will need 4-5 pockets per person, and, conveniently, you can prepare these the day before, leaving the cooking till the very last minute.

When entertaining I prefer to keep the last-minute work to a minimum so that I have time to be with my guests. The main dish of chicken is easy because it needs no attention during cooking: the oven is the master chef. Spinach appears again here, to display its versatility — used in an entirely different way from in the ricotta pockets. Prepare the parcels in advance and put them in to cook when you have finished the first course. Serve with boiled carrots, glazed with a tiny knob of butter.

What better way to anticipate the beautiful days of summer than with this dessert which is simplicity itself to make? The terrine can be made up to a week in advance, leaving just 20 minutes' cooking to make the sauce. Unless you have a sorbetière, making the ices at home will create more work — in this case I suggest you use the excellent ready-made sorbets available, but do check that they have been made only with real fruit.

Overleaf, from left: terrine of sorbets with raspberry sauce; scallops with coriander and ginger; jacket chicken breasts; ricotta and spinach pockets

COUNTDOWN

The day before
• *Prepare the pasta pockets and keep them in the refrigerator.*
• *Make the terrine of sorbets and freeze. Make the raspberry sauce and chill it.*

In the morning
• *Make the sauce for the pasta.*
• *Make the chicken parcels and chill them.*

Just before eating
• *Make the sauce for the scallops. Cook the scallops.*
• *Heat the oven for the chicken parcels.*

After the first course
• *Cook the pasta and reheat the sauce.*

During the second course
• *Cook the chicken parcels.*

SCALLOPS IN THEIR SHELLS WITH CORIANDER AND GINGER SAUCE

SERVES 8

2 tablespoons olive oil

2 teaspoons peanut oil

1 garlic clove, cut into slivers

1cm/½in piece fresh ginger, peeled and cut into fine strips

2 tablespoons soy sauce

few drops of Tabasco sauce, to taste

4 tablespoons beef stock

salt

16 large, fresh scallops in their shells, cleaned

fresh coriander sprigs to garnish

---

1. Make the sauce. Heat the olive and peanut oils in a frying pan and gently fry the garlic and ginger. When the garlic is cooked but not brown, pour in the soy sauce, Tabasco and stock and mix well together.

2. Bring a large pan of slightly salted water to the boil and immerse the scallops in it. As soon as the water boils again, lower the heat and simmer for 5 minutes. Remove the scallops, drain them and serve immediately in the rounded shell, with a spoonful of the sauce and a few coriander sprigs to garnish.

RICOTTA AND SPINACH POCKETS

MAKES ABOUT 32 POCKETS

FOR THE PASTA

250g/8oz wholemeal flour, plus extra for dusting

2 eggs, beaten

pinch of salt

beaten egg, to brush

FOR THE FILLING

200g/7oz fresh spinach, stalks removed

200g/7oz ricotta cheese

freshly grated nutmeg

freshly ground black pepper

FOR THE SAUCE

1kg/2lb fresh tomatoes, blanched and peeled, or 800g/1¾lb can tomatoes

2 tablespoons olive oil

1 garlic clove, finely chopped

4 leaves fresh basil, plus extra to garnish

salt and pepper

40g/1½oz freshly grated Parmesan to serve

---

1. Mix the flour with the eggs, about 4 tablespoons of cold water and the salt. Work the mixture with your hands to give a smooth, but not soft, homogeneous dough. Leave to rest for 1 hour.

2. Meanwhile prepare the filling. Wash the spinach and put in a pan with just the water clinging to the leaves and cook until tender. Squeeze out excess water and chop finely. Mix with the ricotta; season with nutmeg and pepper.

3. If you possess a pasta machine, take some of the dough and, with the help of a little flour, put the dough through the machine, producing a longish sheet of pasta 13-15cm/5½-6in wide and 1mm thick. If you don't have a pasta machine, do the same with a rolling pin, using some flour to avoid sticking.

4. Using a pastry cutter or a glass, cut 8cm/3in diameter rounds from the pasta. Place a teaspoonful of the ricotta mixture just off-centre on each round. Brush the edges with beaten egg. Fold each circle in half and press down round the edge with the prongs of a fork to seal and give a decorative pattern. Dust a tray with some flour and place the pockets on it. Cover with a clean cloth.

5. Make the sauce. Chop the tomatoes coarsely then blend in a liquidizer until smooth. Heat the olive oil in a pan and fry the garlic for 30 seconds until cooked but not browned. Add the tomatoes and roughly torn basil and cook gently for 15 minutes, stirring from time to time. Add the salt and pepper to taste.

6. To serve, bring a large pan of slightly salted water to the boil and add the pockets. Cook for 5-10 minutes (depending on how thinly you have managed to roll the dough). The pockets will rise to the surface when cooked. Drain carefully. Serve immediately with the sauce and grated Parmesan, garnished with basil.

JACKET CHICKEN BREASTS

SERVES 8

3 tablespoons olive oil, plus extra for brushing

800g/1¾lb fresh spinach, washed, dried and trimmed

juice of 2 lemons

3 tablespoons English made mustard

3-4 sprigs tarragon, finely chopped, or 2 teaspoons dried tarragon, plus extra to garnish

salt and freshly ground black pepper

large pinch of freshly grated nutmeg

8 lean boned chicken breasts, weighing about 100g/4oz each

1. Cut out 8 large pieces of aluminium foil and brush each one with oil. Divide half of the spinach leaves between them. Mix together the olive oil, lemon juice, mustard, tarragon, salt, pepper and nutmeg.

2. Spread each chicken breast with this mixture and place on top of the spinach on the foil. Arrange the remaining spinach leaves on the top, pulling them around the chicken to make sure that each piece is completely covered. Bring up the edges of the foil and seal tightly. Chill it if you are not cooking the dish immediately.

3. When ready to cook, heat the oven to 180C/350F/gas 4. Cook for 25 minutes then remove from the foil, slice finely and arrange on dinner plates. Garnish each plate with fresh tarragon.

TERRINE OF SORBETS WITH RASPBERRY SAUCE

SERVES 8

500ml/18fl. oz carton pear sorbet

500ml/18fl. oz carton passion fruit sorbet

500ml/18fl. oz carton blackcurrant sorbet

sprigs of mint to decorate

FOR THE SAUCE

500g/1lb frozen raspberries

4 tablespoons caster sugar

few julienne strips of lemon zest

1. Remove the pear sorbet from the freezer and leave at room temperature to soften until workable. Spread it in an even layer over the base of a 1L/2pt terrine or loaf tin, then return to the freezer to firm up, if necessary, before adding the next layer. Soften the passion fruit sorbet and spread evenly over the pear sorbet. Return to the freezer if necessary. Make a final layer of blackcurrant sorbet in the same way, smooth off, and return to the freezer until firm. If not serving immediately, cover the container and seal.

2. Make the sauce. Put the frozen raspberries in a small pan and leave for 1 hour to defrost. Add the sugar and lemon zest and cook gently for 15 minutes. Strain through a nylon sieve, discard the seeds, and leave to cool.

3. To serve, turn the terrine out on to a plate and cut into 8 slices. Serve on individual plates with a little sauce. Decorate with sprigs of fresh mint.

WINE NOTES

For food that is light, fresh, healthy and delicious the wines must be similar, so go for wines made by modern methods with a view to immediate consumption. Though not everyone associates alcohol with health, there is some evidence that wine taken in moderate measure does lower cholesterol levels and contribute to well-being – as well as good humour.

If you want to go Italian, a bright and light Chardonnay from Alto Adige would suit the scallops, or one of the recently improved Soaves such as Tedeschi's Vigneto Monte Tenda. For a red to accompany the chicken breasts, a light Bardolino or Valpolicella would be excellent, although it is difficult in Britain to get supplies that are sufficiently fresh and fruity unless you go to a specialist outlet. In supermarkets, wines with possibly unfamiliar names (like Refosco or Raboso) will go well if they qualify for the wine guide codes A or B (which designate lighter-bodied wines). Another good thing to look out for would be Italian wine made from the Cabernet Franc grape – Cabernet Franc's redcurrant and grassy flavours are delicious with chicken. If you cannot find an Italian example, I should fall back on Saumur Champigny from the Loire, served lightly chilled for the juiciest and most refreshing effect. Any dessert wine (chilled Asti Spumante would be ideal) should probably best be enjoyed after, rather than with, the sorbets.

SUMMER

*S*ummer brings long lazy days, cool balmy evenings, and fresh produce in abundance. After a hot sticky day, Lyn Hall likes to entertain 'in the cool of the evening'. She offers one of summer's sweetest fish — the pink-fleshed rainbow trout — colourfully combined with tomato and avocado, and an unusual main course of poached veal medallions, with baby vegetables in a beautiful glaze. For Canon John Eley, warm summer Sundays are far from lazy — between services he often cooks and hosts a luncheon party, taking advantage of summer's bounty: salmon married to prawns in a mousse, a medley of the season's new vegetables with his main course, and a rich blackcurrant sauce to offset a refreshing lime sorbet.

Frances Bissell gives classic summer ingredients an original cloak: courgettes are partnered with fresh dill in a chilled soup, and that king of summer fish — salmon or, almost better, salmon trout — is masked in a watercress cream then tucked into a crisp filo case. And what more perfect ending to a leisurely lunch can there be than individual little summer puddings?

Maddalena Bonino also favours fish for summer dinners, adding a Moorish touch to her trio of fish with a delicate hazelnut sauce, while carrots are given a delicate air by being stripped into fine ribbons. Always impressive are featherlight home-made biscuits, especially when accompanied with a cooling zabaione and mango mousse.

In the heat of the summer, barbecues are perhaps the most popular event; give them a new look with Suzy Benghiat's wonderfully exotic Middle Eastern dishes — a true Arabian Nights' feast . . . Antony Kwok takes us further east, and puts our summer garden vegetables into tiny filo nests, reminiscent of those fragile tea bowls of the Orient, while that most delicate of teas — jasmine — is enticingly turned into a sorbet. As autumn approaches and the air turns chilly, Frances Bissell adds a warmth to the flavours of summer with a scallop and saffron sauce for little parcels of pasta, and a rich chocolate sauce for a hot mint soufflé.

Lyn Hall

IN THE COOL OF THE EVENING

Celebrate the beginning of summer with this simple but stunning menu created by Lyn Hall

---

Trout salad with tomato and avocado vinaigrette

Poached veal medallions with glazed baby vegetables

Lemon ice cream in a gingersnap basket

Summer is my favourite time of the year, because so many delicious ingredients are at their best. Celebrate the start of the better weather with this dinner party menu which marries ambition and practicality.

The challenge is that the veal for the main course is cooked at the last moment, but this should not present too much of a problem because the starter, the dessert and the vegetables to accompany the veal can all be prepared well in advance of the meal.

The summery pink and green first course of trout salad is designed to look delicately attractive on the plate, but don't be deceived: it has plenty of flavour.

For the main course the veal medallions are cooked rather differently from usual. Many people think that the only way to treat small cuts of meat is to sauté them, but for this dish they are poached in a good stock which you make yourself. Try this method for other delicate cuts, such as beef fillet or breast of chicken or duck.

As for the stock, it truly is worth taking the time to make it. The aromatic result will probably put you off commercial stock cubes for life. Prepare it when you have other things to do in the kitchen and it can, for the most part, bubble away quietly on its own.

To go with the veal serve the tiniest of early season vegetables: crisp baby carrots, potatoes, courgettes, haricots verts and mangetouts, all glazed like the meat.

In the countdown I suggest you cook the veal just before sitting down to dinner. However, I like cooking at the last possible moment and, as the veal takes at most five minutes to poach, I would finish what is essentially a last-minute dish after the first course, directly before serving the meat.

After the salad to start and the abundance of vegetables to follow, I resisted the temptation to close the dinner with a dessert based on fruit salad. Instead I suggest a luscious home-made ice cream, which is spectacularly presented. The garnish is tiny sprigs of seasonal redcurrants.

If this is your first dinner party of summer, that in itself is an excuse to celebrate, so why not serve pink champagne? It would certainly look and taste wonderfully stylish.

Alternatively, serve white wine throughout the meal. Start with a chilled white port for an aperitif, offer a Riesling from Alsace to accompany the trout, and a St-Véran to go with the veal.

Avoid serving any wine with the dessert. Lemon and ice cream both numb the palate, so together they will certainly not complement any wine. Wait until after the third course and pass round a bottle of a liqueur such as Amaretto, cognac or Cointreau.

COUNTDOWN

Up to a week ahead

• *Make the lemon ice cream. Freeze then shape into balls and refreeze. The veal stock can be made and frozen well ahead too.*

The day before

• *Defrost the veal stock and divide in half; refrigerate one portion for poaching the veal. Boil the remaining stock to reduce for the sauce; reduce the Madeira and combine the two, then strain for the sauce. Do all your shopping.*

In the morning

• *Make the gingersnap baskets and store in an airtight tin.*
• *Bake the trout in their paper parcels. Part-cook the vinaigrette and leave for the flavours to steep. Wash and dry the salad leaves; put in bags to crisp in the salad drawer of the refrigerator.*
• *Prepare and cook the vegetables, refresh and set them on a wire rack to dry. Reserve the cooking water.*
• *Chill the wines.*

An hour before

• *Warm the serving dish and plates for the main course.*
• *Put the gingersnap basket for the dessert on a serving platter.*
• *Prepare a pan for reheating the vegetables by reducing the reserved cooking liquid and making the glaze.*
• *Thicken the stock reserved for the veal sauce with arrowroot; leave in the saucepan, ready to reheat.*
• *Arrange the salad and trout on plates. Sieve the vinaigrette and add the avocado and tomato.*
• *Have a drink with your guests.* ▶

TROUT SALAD WITH TOMATO AND AVOCADO VINAIGRETTE

Look for large paper bags in which to cook the fish, or make your own parcels using greaseproof paper or foil. Baking fish *en papillote* like this is a wonderful way to keep it moist if you are going to eat it cold.

SERVES 6

FOR THE TROUT
3 × 250g/8oz pink-fleshed rainbow trout, gutted
½ lemon, cut into 6 slices
6 sprigs parsley
oil for greasing
FOR THE VINAIGRETTE
1 shallot or small onion, finely chopped
1 whole unpeeled garlic clove
16 coriander seeds, lightly crushed
6 tablespoons extra virgin olive oil
2 tablespoons sherry vinegar
1 tablespoon chopped chives
2 tablespoons chopped parsley
salt and freshly ground pepper
1 medium-sized avocado, the flesh diced
2 fresh ripe tomatoes, skinned, seeded and diced
FOR THE SALAD
50g/2oz lettuce leaves
50g/2oz curly endive
100g/4oz cucumber, peeled

1. Start preparing the dish by cooking the fish. Heat the oven to 180C/350F/gas 4.

2. Season the cavities of the fish then stuff them with the lemon slices and parsley. If you are going to cook the fish in paper bags, grease the insides of the bags lightly with oil and place on a baking sheet before inserting the trout. Alternatively, cut a double thickness of greaseproof paper or foil big enough to cover each fish. Grease these with oil, place on a baking sheet, and put one trout in the centre of each. Pull up the edges of the paper or foil and twist them together over the fish to make baggy parcels. Twist the ends together firmly.

3. Bake the fish for 10-15 minutes. To test whether they are cooked open the bag and part the flesh behind the head — it should be opaque.

4. While the fish is baking put the first seven vinaigrette ingredients in the top pan of a double boiler with 4 tablespoons water. Heat the liquid thoroughly (this helps the flavours to infuse), then set aside to cool.

5. Remove the fish from the paper bags or parcels and leave at room temperature until completely cold.

6. Skin the cold fish.

7. Slide a sharp knife into the fish horizontally, on top of the backbone. Remove the top fillets, then lift out the backbone to release the bottom fillets. Then, with your fingers, gently pull the fish into rough V-shaped pieces, working from the head end and using the natural flake of the fish. Reserve the fish pieces in a cool place.

8. Discard outside leaves of the lettuce and endive and wash and dry the leaves you need. Slice the peeled cucumber very thinly.

9. Up to an hour before serving divide the salad leaves and cucumber between six plates, making a mound in the centre of each. Prop the trout pieces, points upwards, round the salad leaves to form cone-shaped salads. Season with salt and freshly ground pepper. Cover loosely with cling film if the dishes are to stand, and reserve in a cool place.

10. Pour the vinaigrette through a muslin-lined sieve (or a tea-strainer). Peel and dice the avocado and tomatoes and stir the dice into the vinaigrette dressing.

11. When ready to serve, remove cling film from salads and dribble vinaigrette over the salad leaves and the trout. Make sure some of the avocado dice lie against the trout as they make an attractive colour combination.

Note:

Omit the cucumber if you have a choice of pretty summer salad leaves, such as dark green lamb's lettuce or red-edged oak-leaf lettuce (but not red radicchio, which clashes with the trout).

GOLDEN VEAL STOCK

Although you have to buy the bones and meat trimmings for this, the tiny amount of vegetables needed can easily be drawn from the basics in the refrigerator. They don't have to be of the best quality. Don't be tempted, though, to put in extra vegetable trimmings: if you do, you may well find they overshadow the clear and distinctive taste of veal.

Stocks should be heated and chilled quickly, to stop them going off.

MAKES ABOUT 1L/2pt

1.5kg/3¼lb veal bones (knuckle and shin), chopped by the butcher into small pieces
500g/1lb lean beef trimmings
40g/1½oz cooked ham
2 teaspoons each chopped leek, onion, carrot, tomato, all in cubes
1 teaspoon chopped celery leaves
150ml/¼pt white wine
1 bouquet garni, made with 1 garlic clove, ½ bay leaf, several parsley stalks, small sprig of thyme, all wrapped up in a leek leaf
5 peppercorns

1. Use an oven heated to 225C-240C/425F-475F/gas 7-9. Put the bones and beef in a roasting tin and bake for 15 minutes until brown, turning often.

2. Put the bones, beef trimmings, the ham and the vegetables into a large saucepan with the wine, bouquet garni and peppercorns, then rinse out the roasting tin into the pan with 2L/3½pt water. Bring to the boil, skim, lower the heat and simmer, uncovered, for 3-4 hours. Add extra water when necessary so that the bones are always well submerged. Skim frequently.

3. Line a sieve with muslin and strain the stock. When it reaches room temperature, remove the fat with a spoon. Chill, then remove any remaining fat.

Note:

You need double these quantities for the following recipe, so either use 2 pans or make in 2 batches.

Countdown (continued)

Ten minutes before

• *Brown the veal medallions and strain the pan juices. Poach the medallions in stock, then remove to a warm place.*

• *Pour the vinaigrette over the salad and serve.*

After the first course

• *Move the ice cream from the freezer to the refrigerator.*

• *Heat the glaze and toss the vegetables in it.*

• *Reheat the sauce very gently, strain it and dish up the main course.*

After the main course

• *Put the lemon ice cream balls in the gingersnap basket and decorate with redcurrant sprigs.*

POACHED VEAL MEDALLIONS WITH GLAZED BABY VEGETABLES

Succulent circles of veal are given a glossy deep brown sauce and served with a selection of crisp, jewel-bright glazed baby vegetables (see the following recipe).

SERVES 6

FOR THE SAUCE
1L/2pt golden veal stock (see previous recipe)
200ml/7fl. oz Madeira
salt and black pepper
1 teaspoon arrowroot
FOR THE MEAT
6×75g/3oz veal medallions cut from veal fillet, each about 4cm/1½in thick and tied round with string
salt and black pepper
40ml/1½fl. oz Madeira
1L/2pt golden veal stock, for poaching
glazed baby vegetables (see following recipe)

1. For the sauce, reduce the stock by slow boiling to 450ml/¾pt. In another saucepan reduce the Madeira to 50ml/2fl. oz. Combine the two in the larger pan and season to taste. Strain through a muslin-lined sieve.

2. Mix the arrowroot with a little water. Add some of the hot liquid, whisk it in, then pour into the remainder of the reduced stock and boil briefly to thicken, whisking all the time. If over-boiled the sauce will become thin again.

3. To cook the veal, season both sides of the medallions with salt and freshly ground black pepper then, in a sturdy preheated pan (with no fat), brown them on both sides until just golden. Remove from the pan.

4. Pour 40ml/1½fl. oz Madeira into the pan, mixing in any pan juices. Boil hard until reduced to a syrupy glaze, then add it to the sauce.

5. Put the stock for poaching into a roasting tin or pan large enough to take the medallions in a single layer with at least 5cm/2in depth of liquid. Bring to the boil. Add the medallions to the stock and immediately reduce to a simmer. Cook the veal for 2-3 minutes, until just spongy to the touch. The medallions should still be fairly pink inside. Remove the medallions, cover them with foil and keep them warm in a very low oven. (Use the stock to make soup.)

6. Reheat the sauce (just to boiling point) and strain it through a sieve lined with muslin: this will make it smooth and glossy.

7. Place the medallions on a warmed, shallow serving dish and spoon a little sauce over the meat. Arrange the glazed vegetables round the veal and serve immediately. Serve the remaining hot sauce in a gravy boat.

GLAZED BABY VEGETABLES

Take advantage of the new season's delicate vegetables; the glaze emphasizes their natural sweetness.

SERVES 6

18 baby new potatoes, scrubbed and scraped
12 baby carrots, peeled, with 2.5cm/1in of green tops still on
250g/8oz baby courgettes, cut in half lengthways and sliced evenly
350g/12oz haricots verts, topped and tailed
100g/4oz mange-touts, topped and tailed
50g/2oz clarified butter
40g/1½oz caster sugar

1. Bring a large pan of lightly salted water to the boil. Add the potatoes and simmer for 10-15 minutes, depending on size, until almost cooked. After 5 minutes or so add the carrots; cook for 5-10 minutes depending on size. When these vegetables are ready, remove from pan with a slotted spoon. Plunge them into a big bowl of iced water for a minute to refresh them. Drain and dry on a wire rack.

2. Using the same water, cook the courgettes and haricots verts for 2 minutes, then add the mange-touts and cook for 1 more minute. Remove all the vegetables and refresh and dry them in the same way.

3. Use the vegetable liquid to prepare the glaze. Take two large ladlesful (about 600ml/1pt) and put it into a roasting tin or shallow pan large enough to hold all the vegetables in a single layer. Boil down the stock to a depth of 2.5cm/1in and then add the clarified butter and sugar. Boil down again until the liquid is 1cm/½in deep, just enough to coat the vegetables when turned in the glaze. Reserve it ready for reheating the vegetables at the last moment before serving.

4. When ready to serve, quickly reheat the glaze and add the vegetables, starting with the potatoes and carrots. Shake the pan gently for 1 minute then add the remaining vegetables and coat them in the boiling glaze.

Note:

Clarified butter is one of those useful things to have in the refrigerator when you are giving a dinner party. It is less likely to burn or smell at high temperatures, nor does it discolour. It also goes a long way.

To make, start with twice as much butter as your recipes require. Do use unsalted butter if possible as this has far fewer impurities in it. Heat the butter gently until the froth subsides, then pass it into a bowl through a double thickness of muslin which will retain the impurities. The butter should now be crystal clear. It keeps very well in the refrigerator.

LEMON ICE CREAM IN A GINGERSNAP BASKET

This is a great finale to the meal and it *is* easy to make. It has the added attraction that it can be made ahead and assembled just before serving.

Measure the ingredients for the basket with great care: the correct proportions are vital. The quantities given are for two baskets — one for practice, one to serve.

SERVES 6
FOR THE ICE CREAM
450ml/¾pt double cream
300ml/½pt single cream
4 large egg yolks
freshly grated zest of 2 lemons
250ml/9fl. oz lemon juice
160g/5½oz caster sugar
FOR THE GINGERSNAP
50g/2oz golden syrup
50g/2oz caster sugar
50g/2oz butter
50g/2oz plain flour
1 teaspoon ground ginger
finely grated zest of 1 lemon
a little soft butter for greasing
TO GARNISH
sprigs of redcurrants

1. Start by making the ice cream. Turn the freezer, or the freezing compartment in a refrigerator, to its lowest setting.

2. Whisk all the cream together until thick. Whisk in 2 egg yolks.

3. Grate the lemon zest, squeeze the juice and make up the juice with water to 250ml/9fl. oz. Stir in the sugar and remaining 2 egg yolks, then incorporate with the cream mixture. Stir until smooth.

4. Turn into a metal container and freeze until the mixture becomes slushy round the edges — about 2 hours. Turn out and beat (a food processor does this splendidly). Return to the freezer then beat again after ¾ hour. When smooth, cover and freeze until firm. Freeze for a further hour before the next step and clear a space in the freezer for a tray.

5. Using a scoop dipped in hot water,

WINE NOTES

Among the grandes marques *of champagne the two that stand out for the quality and value of their pink wines are Pol Roger and Laurent-Perrier. A smaller house that consistently produces delicious wine with a really marked flavour of wood strawberries is Roland Fliniaux. Pink champagnes from the supermarkets are notably cheaper, but far from consistent in quality.*

White port is a less appreciated aperitif, and frankly, there are not too many to choose from. The cheapest tend to be somewhat sweet, and it is worth paying the little extra for something tangy and dry. On hot summer days this is delicious chilled as an aperitif – try it with mineral or tonic water, a twist of orange, or ice.

Unlike German Rieslings, the Alsace Rieslings that Lyn Hall suggests to accompany the trout are steely, bone dry wines of great distinction and refreshing acidity. This is a good choice if you enjoy the sharpness of lemon with trout. Top names of reliable houses include Trimbach, Beyer and Hugel, but note also that the Alsace co-operatives are some of the best in France.

St-Véran, adjoining Beaujolais and formerly much sold as Beaujolais Blanc, is one of the best value cheaper white burgundies – a taste-alike for Pouilly-Fuissé which international enthusiasm tends to price out of sight. The wines of Corsin, Raymond, Georges Duboeuf and Marcel Vincent are dependable, as is the co-operative de Chaintre and the Producteurs de Prisse. ▶

Wine Notes (continued)

Alternatives would be other Mâconnais appellations like Mâcon-Viré, Mâcon-Lugny, or Mâcon-Clessé; or white burgundies from the much improved Côte Chalonnaise districts of Rully and Montagny. Alas, even with these less prestigious names, white burgundy is never cheap.

Lemon ice cream in a gingersnap basket

scoop 13 or more perfect balls from the ice cream. Set them on greaseproof paper on an upside-down tray (it's easier to remove them later) and freeze them hard, then cover with cling film and freeze until required.

6. Next, make the gingersnap basket. Heat the oven to 200C/400F/gas 6. Choose a deep pudding basin with a top diameter of about 16cm/6½in for shaping the basket.

7. Warm the syrup, sugar and butter over a gentle heat. Sift the flour and ginger together and stir into the pan with the grated lemon zest. Remove

immediately from the heat and cool until you can handle it easily.

8. Lavishly butter 2 baking sheets at least 30cm/12in square, turned upside down for easy removal of the gingersnaps. Then, with wet fingers, take half the mixture (75g/3oz), and press it into a circle on one sheet as thin as it will go without holes (it will spread when cooked). Bake for 5-6 minutes until golden brown round the edges. Keep watching!

9. Remove from the oven and leave for a minute or so, until the snap is just firm enough to move. Then, with a long palette knife, remove the snap from the sheet and drape it over the inverted pudding basin, with the lacy topside still facing up. If the snap won't model properly (it may be too brittle or have hardened on the tray) return it *briefly* to the oven.

10. Allow the basket to cool before taking it off the mould. Make a second basket the same way. Keep the baskets in a deep airtight tin in a cool place until needed (but no longer than 5 hours). If possible, place the baskets on a rack above a good sprinkling of silica gel crystals (see note). These will keep them crisp. Use whichever basket was the more successful.

To assemble:

11. Trim the basket with scissors if it looks untidy, and arrange on a platter.

12. Just before serving the main course move the ice cream from the freezer to the refrigerator to soften. Use one ball to test for softness.

13. After the main course remove the ice cream balls from the tray (with a hot knife if necessary), and place them in the gingersnap basket.

14. Serve two scoops of ice cream per guest, with a piece of gingersnap basket and a few redcurrants.

Note:

Silica gel crystals absorb moisture from the air and are often put in the bottom of camera or binoculars cases to keep them dry. They are also ideal for keeping biscuits crisp.

Canon John Eley

SUNDAY LUNCH AT THE VICARAGE

Between taking the morning service and baptisms in the afternoon, Canon John Eley often entertains with a lunch party. His menu is simple with the emphasis on fresh ingredients

---

Salmon and prawn mousse

Chicken and bacon casserole
Baked cherry tomatoes
Steamed cubes of marrow
New potatoes, baby turnips

Lime champagne sorbet with blackcurrant sauce

When organizing a lunch at the Vicarage, deciding what to offer and who to invite involves careful and tactful planning. At a stroke, lunch needs to be an enjoyable diversion, in an otherwise demanding life which often mixes business with pleasure.

I abhor those occasions when I have been invited, as what seemed on the surface a purely pleasant gesture, to find that there was a 'reason', other than being entertained by my amiable host. But that does not mean an occasion cannot be used. I often invite young couples who are thinking about getting wed or, indeed, are already engaged, to lunch with us. At the same time, I invite a family with four or more children, so that the young can see the benefits of 'family life'.

I've enjoyed many feasts at vicarage dining tables. I learned a lot about cooking in vicarages before I was ordained, indeed, before I even considered the possibility of being ordained. We had a lot of fun in the process, especially doing it on a limited budget. One thing I have learned is that it's not what is provided to eat, but the company who share the repast with you, that is the important thing.

Life at a vicarage affords a large menu of different types of people, and we mix guests in a way that

COUNTDOWN

• *The world's view of Sunday as the vicar's busiest day is simply not true. He will be in certain places at set times: church services at 8am and 10am; baptisms at 3pm; evensong at 6pm. Given the fact that he is human and has to eat, an unmarried vicar has to spend some time in the kitchen.*

The day before

• *Saturdays are a slightly different kettle of fish. There are the weddings, and it is the couple's special day so you have to be at your best. But you also have to shop.*

• *I usually know what I want before I go, although I don't make a shopping list, and I get infuriated when they change things around in the shop so I have to start looking again. On the way back we have a very good roadside greengrocer selling some of the finest vegetables from the Vale of Evesham.*

• *One of the pleasures of working from and living in the vicarage is that I can start some work in the kitchen, get fed up or frustrated, and then go to the study to work on the sermon. When I have a mental block I can return to the equally creative activity in the kitchen.*

• *I would make the starter in the morning. Time is of the essence, as the telephone always rings at the most crucial moment; so the portable telephone goes everywhere with me. The preparation time for the salmon and prawn mousses should be an hour including cooking, plus the chilling overnight.* ▶

would be almost impossible in any other group. There has often been a skinhead and a bishop at the same table and they seem to get on well.

When I was a curate at Sherborne in Dorset, I lived in a three-bedroomed semi. As the junior member of the clergy team, I took an interest in the young people of the Parish. We had many noisy parties but occasionally, when they were older, we would have large lunch parties and squeeze up to 24 people into the dining area, sitting down to a proper meal. Surprisingly, they took to this idea well and these lunches became a highlight of the school holidays. The teenagers would always dress up for the occasion and make an event of eating a meal together around the large, carefully arranged tables.

Summer holidays provided the opportunity for alfresco feasts in the small garden, much to the amusement of our neighbours. They were formal but very friendly occasions, when we could chew the cud of life, and some decent food. The meal was usually followed by a long ramble into the Dorset countryside, whence they would return with rosy cheeks, and usually soaking wet, having jumped in the river to cool off. Then it was time for tea before they all changed and went off to the disco or local hostelry for the rest of the evening.

Sitting around a table together at least once a day must be one of the things that builds up family life. Not just sharing the quick refuelling type of meal, but also the more leisurely eating times. There are, after all, two kinds of meal: the refuelling stop and the pleasant social experience when we can enter into a new relationship with one another. Eating is one of the most private things we do in public. I am sure if we spent more time talking over our own and the world's problems at meal times it would be a better place for us all to live in.

The pleasure in the event starts at the early stages of planning and shopping. I enjoy shopping and selecting the ingredients with care, especially when I am going to entertain. I'm a great believer in really good, fresh ingredients and dishes that do not demand a great deal of time in preparation. There are far too many compromises made in the food industry so that profits can be maintained. I believe that generations to come will pay the price with their health for our eating too many convenience foods.

With the casserole, sticking to my golden rule of simplicity, I would serve new potatoes and steamed cubes of marrow.

I would suggest Meursault and Auxey-Duresses to drink with the meal. I seldom serve sherry as an aperitif, but I always enjoy Kenyan coffee afterwards.

Let's get back to gathering in the kitchen as a family and joining in the process of cooking and home-making. And let's get round the table again with family and friends to enjoy good fare and the pleasures of life together.

SALMON AND PRAWN MOUSSE

SERVES 10

25g/1oz unsalted butter
pinch of ground mace
250g/8oz fresh salmon steak, skinned and boned
250g/8oz fresh or frozen peeled cooked prawns
4 large egg yolks
300ml/½pt double cream
salt and ground black pepper
75g/3oz Gruyère cheese
red pepper to garnish

1. Heat the oven to 180C/350F/gas 4. Soak the *Church Times* in hot water until thoroughly sodden. Place it at the bottom of a large shallow roasting tin and cover with about 5cm/2in water.

Heat until the water simmers.

2. Liberally butter 10 ramekins (about 100ml/3½fl. oz) and sprinkle each with ground mace. Place a piece of salmon and a few prawns in each ramekin and stand them in a cool place.

3. Meanwhile, make the sauce: whisk the egg yolks until they are really creamy and then add the cream. Mix well until blended. Season with salt and freshly ground black pepper, then strain the cream sauce through a nylon sieve. Gently pour this mixture over the fish in the ramekins.

4. Remove the roasting tin from the oven and carefully place the ramekins in the simmering water. Cover the top of the roasting tin loosely with foil and put the tin in the oven. Cook for 30 minutes or until just set.

5. Remove the tin from the oven and leave the ramekins to cool standing in the water. When cold, cover them with cling film and place in the refrigerator. Leave them to chill for several hours or overnight. Put 10 small plates in the refrigerator to chill.

6. On the day of deliverance, about 20 minutes before serving, run a knife round each ramekin and turn out on to the chilled plates. Finely grate the Gruyère and sprinkle over the mousses. Decorate with sliced red pepper.

CHICKEN AND BACON CASSEROLE

SERVES 10

20 chicken thighs, skinned
20 rashers smoked back bacon, without rind
40g/1½oz unsalted butter
2 large onions, chopped
salt and black pepper
3 tablespoons freshly chopped French tarragon or 2 heaped teaspoons dried tarragon
1L/2pt home-made chicken stock
300g/10oz button mushrooms
25g/1oz cornflour for thickening (optional)
75ml/3fl. oz double cream (optional)

1. This really couldn't be easier to make. I always use an enormous sauté pan for this dish; it travels well to the table for serving. Wrap each thigh with

Countdown (continued)

• *In between the weddings in the afternoon, I set the table for Sunday lunch. I suppose it is a bit of a ritual; I like to set the table and close the door on the dining room until we are ready to go in on Sunday morning to add the final touches. Leaving the dining room door closed lets it obtain an air of calm!*

• *Last thing at night, I prepare the sorbet and the sauce, making sure that I have all the dishes and plates in the refrigerator chilling for the 'morrow. I find that making the dessert is a good way to unwind after writing the sermon.*

In the morning

• *I always rise early on Sunday morning. Before the 8am service I have a cup of coffee and prepare the vegetables, making sure I don't touch the onions: it is not appreciated if my hands smell of onions when I'm handling holy things.*

• *After the service, it is breakfast, and there's time to read the papers and line up all the ingredients for the casserole before going off to the 10am service.*

• *We have coffee in the church hall after the service. But I am back in the kitchen by noon, giving me enough time to put together the main dish. At 12.45pm when my guests arrive, I pop in the vegetables, and then we are ready for drinks. We usually eat at 1pm or a little after, but no matter what time I sit down at the table, I will only have the chance to taste one dish when the telephone will ring: 'Ah Vicar, I knew I would catch you in . . .'. No peace for the wicked.*

a rasher of bacon, with the 'eye' of the rasher on the outer part of the wrap.

2. Gently heat the butter in the large sauté pan and add the chopped onions. Cover with the lid and allow to cook until the onions are soft. Sprinkle with a little salt and freshly ground black pepper and cook for a further 1-2 minutes. Add the dried herbs to the pan if using.

3. Add the wrapped chicken joints to the pan with the stock, making sure it just covers the chicken. Sprinkle in the fresh tarragon if using; cover the pan and simmer for 20 minutes. Slice the mushrooms and add them to the sauté pan; cook for a further 30 minutes.

4. Before serving, remove the chicken joints from the pan and keep warm under foil. Stir the cornflour into the cream; stir into the juices, over a low heat, to thicken the sauce.

Baked cherry tomatoes

Heat the oven to 190C/375F/gas 5. Score about 20 cherry tomatoes around their middles (to prevent bursting). Pack the tomatoes into a Swiss roll tin. Pour over 40g/1½ oz melted butter and bake for 10 minutes.

It is good to know that the canonical stipend can still stretch to white burgundy, and the Canon's choice is a classic one. Meursault is many people's ideal white burgundy, with its strong nuts and honey-spice aroma, rich unctuous texture and long lingering flavour. Auxey-Duresses is its slightly more modest and less expensive neighbour. But a good straight Meursault is likely to be £15 a bottle and the more concentrated premier cru wines may be £20.

One possible economical substitute is Bourgogne Aligoté, made from Burgundy's inferior workhorse grape variety: you may be able to find a wine from a Meursault grower. Otherwise, for a bottle under £10, one may have to look for white burgundy taste-alikes among Chardonnays from other countries – the likeliest sources being California and Australia.

LIME CHAMPAGNE SORBET WITH BLACKCURRANT SAUCE

SERVES 10

500g/1lb caster sugar

thinly pared zest and juice of 6 limes

½ bottle champagne

freshly grated coconut or finely pared lime zest to decorate

FOR THE SAUCE

1kg/2lb blackcurrants, defrosted if frozen

250g/8oz icing sugar, sifted

1. Put the sugar in a heavy-based pan with 300ml/½pt water, and dissolve over a very low heat. Add the lime zest, bring to the boil and simmer for 5 minutes. Strain the mixture and leave to cool completely. Add the lime juice and the champagne.

2. Use an ice cream maker, or pour the sorbet mixture into a chilled freezer container, cover and freeze for several hours or until beginning to freeze round the edges. Tip the semi-frozen sorbet into a food processor or whisk in a chilled bowl. Return to the freezer and leave until frozen. The sorbet is soft enough to serve straight from the freezer.

3. To make the sauce: wash and string the currants if fresh and place them in a heavy-based pan. Add 600ml/1pt water and bring gently to the boil; simmer for 15 minutes, then immediately force through a nylon sieve and discard the pips and skin. Pour the juice into a food processor or blender and set at a high speed. Gradually add the icing sugar. Pour into a glass jug and leave to chill; also chill 10 serving plates.

4. When ready to serve, pour a little of the blackcurrant sauce on to each plate and spoon 2 scoops of sorbet on to the centre of each. Decorate with freshly grated coconut if available, or finely pared lime zest.

Frances Bissell

A LEISURELY LUNCH

Pray for a perfect summer day, then enjoy a lingering lunch on the lawn with Frances Bissell's deliciously pretty cold menu

---

Cheese clafoutis

Chilled courgette and dill soup

Salmon in filo pastry with watercress cream
Salad of mixed summer greens
Tomato and basil salad

Wheel of brie

Summer pudding

This meal is for one of those English summer days when you know it is safe to plan to eat outdoors. Sit on the lawn, on the balcony or perhaps make it into a very elaborate picnic, provided you have plenty of fetchers and carriers!

A garden room, conservatory, summer house, folly, or open French windows would provide equally fitting settings for a meal that is unashamedly summery and pretty.

I have tried to make the most of fresh herbs because they are at their most fragrant, having had a good helping of summer sun to develop their aromatic oils. In contrast to the various shades of green I have brought in the pinks and richer reds of salmon, summer fruit and gloriously ripe tomatoes.

The pink and green theme can be picked up in what you serve to drink. I don't see this as being an entirely serious meal — somehow eating outside is always slightly frivolous, so grand wines would be a little out of place.

COUNTDOWN

The day before

• *Make the summer pudding and weight the top. Leave overnight.*
• *Make and chill the courgette and dill soup.*
• *Make ice for the fruit cup if needed.*
• *Make the batter for the clafoutis.*
• *Move the filo pastry from freezer to refrigerator to defrost overnight.*

In the morning

• *Make and bake the salmon in filo pastry. Allow 1 hour for cooking and at least 1 hour for cooling.*
• *Toast the walnuts for the salad of summer greens in the oven as it cools.*

Two hours before lunch

• *Chill white wine or open red.*
• *Make the tomato and basil salad and leave at room temperature for the flavours to blend.*
• *Wash and pick over the mixed salad leaves and put them in a polythene bag in the bottom of the refrigerator to crisp.*
• *Make the vinaigrette in the bottom of your salad bowl.*

One hour before lunch

• *Heat the oven and make and bake the clafoutis.*
• *Unmould the summer pudding.*
• *Make the fruit cup.*

Just before the meal

• *Serve the hot clafoutis with drinks.*
• *Garnish the chilled soup with dill and a swirl of cream.*
• *Beat the vinaigrette to reform the emulsion and toss the mixed salad greens. Sprinkle with chopped toasted walnuts.*

Wine lightened with herbs, fruit and soda water would be fun, refreshing and delicious. I would serve a jug of sparkling dry white, perhaps a Saumur or a Blanquette de Limoux, or another *méthode champenoise*, with long curled strips of cucumber peel, a handful of fresh mint leaves, a few bruised blackcurrant leaves, scented geranium leaves and some borage if possible.

I would also serve some red, again in a large crystal jug with a few soft fruits steeped in it — lightly crushed raspberries, redcurrants, even blackcurrants — and topped up with sparkling mineral water.

Which wine to choose? A fairly full one, not too thin, and firm. Perhaps a Côtes du Roussillon, a Minervois, a Vin de Pays de l'Hérault or possibly Saint Chinian. Turning from France to Spain, a young Rioja would be pleasant served in a jug like this.

As to the choice of fish, I usually prefer salmon trout, now sold as sea trout, but if my fishmonger has some River Tay salmon, it's very hard to resist it. This is purely a matter of personal preference.

Home-grown soft fruit is at its best in early summer, so let's put aside the Mediterranean peaches, apricots and nectarines for a while and enjoy the quintessential English dessert — summer pudding. I find it quite delicious made with wholemeal bread. Strawberries are not traditionally included, but since they are often available and usually a little cheaper than raspberries, I have suggested using them here.

The beauty of this meal is that you can prepare it in advance. Indeed, many of the flavours improve by being left — overnight in the case of the summer pudding. However, I wouldn't recommend cooking the salmon in pastry the day before because you will have to put it in the refrigerator. Cook it in the morning and it will be cold by lunchtime.

CHEESE CLAFOUTIS

Clafoutis is traditionally a pudding made with cherries and served at harvest time in the Limousin area of France. The batter mixture adapts perfectly to these little cheesy *bouchées* which you can serve warm with drinks before lunch.

MAKES 24 INDIVIDUAL CLAFOUTIS

50g/2oz plain flour
pinch of salt
2 eggs, beaten
300ml/½pt milk
75g/3oz Gruyère or other hard cheese

1. Sift the flour and salt together. Make a well in the centre and add the eggs.

Mix to a cream, gradually adding the milk until you have a smooth batter.

2. Grate half the cheese as finely as possible. This is important, otherwise it will form lumps. Add to the batter and leave to stand for at least 2 hours. Cut the remaining cheese into tiny cubes.

3. About 45 minutes before you want to serve the clafoutis, heat the oven to 200C/400F/gas 6 and thoroughly butter or oil 2 bun tins (each with 12 compartments). Pour a tablespoon of batter into each hollow and sprinkle a few cubes of cheese on top.

4. Bake for 20 minutes in the upper half of the oven, until they are quite brown and puffed up. Remove, and cool them slightly. The clafoutis will sink, but this won't affect the flavour in any way.

CHILLED COURGETTE AND DILL SOUP

SERVES 8

700g/1½lb courgettes
1 small onion
2 garlic cloves
1 tablespoon olive oil
1L/2pt stock
1 teaspoon cornflour
150ml/¼pt single cream, plus extra to serve if wished
salt and pepper
1 bunch dill — about 2 tablespoons, roughly chopped

1. Wash the courgettes, trim off the ends, then grate the flesh. Peel the onion and garlic and chop them finely.

2. Heat the olive oil in a heavy-based pan and stir in the vegetables to coat them. Pour on 150ml/¼pt stock and cook, covered, for 6-10 minutes, until the vegetables are soft. Don't overcook or the lovely green colour will be lost.

3. Mix the cornflour with a little more stock and add it to the vegetables. Cook it until you can no longer taste the raw flour.

4. Leave to cool for 10 minutes, then stir in the cream, season to taste (if you're using a stock cube you won't need salt), and add almost all the dill, saving a few sprigs for decoration.

5. Purée in a blender in 3 or 4 batches, adding a portion of the remaining stock to each batch.

6. Pour into a decorative bowl and chill. Just before serving garnish with the reserved dill and perhaps a swirl of single cream.

SALMON IN FILO PASTRY WITH WATERCRESS CREAM

For this you will need an ovenproof dish approximately 25 × 35cm/10 × 14in, and about 4cm/1½in deep.

SERVES 8

100g/4oz watercress
600ml/1pt boiling water
8 size 3 eggs
50ml/2fl. oz single cream
100ml/3½fl. oz fish stock
salt and black pepper
100ml/3½fl. oz olive oil for brushing on the layers of pastry. Any unused oil can be added to the salad vinaigrette
400g/14oz packet filo pastry
1 level tablespoon cumin seed
1.5kg/3¼lb fillet of salmon or salmon trout, skinned
1 tablespoon lemon juice

1. Put the watercress in a sieve or colander. Rinse under running water, removing any damaged leaves and tough stalks. Blanch by leaving it in the sieve and pouring over the boiling water.
2. Put the watercress, eggs, cream, fish stock, salt and pepper in a blender and purée until you have a pale green cream.
3. In a non-stick frying pan or large-based non-stick saucepan cook the mixture gently as if you were preparing scrambled eggs. Stir constantly. Once the mixture begins to 'set' remove from the heat and stir for a minute or two longer. The mixture will have the consistency of double cream, and will be easier to handle at the next stage than if it were completely liquid. Allow the mixture to cool.
4. Brush the inside of the dish lightly with olive oil. (If you were serving the dish hot, melted butter would be fine, but it would congeal as the pie cooled, and so oil is better for the cold version.)
5. Heat the oven to 190-200C/375-400F/gas 5-6. Gently unroll the filo pastry, put a whole sheet over the oiled dish and press into place to line the dish. Brush oil all over the pastry, even on the

overlapping edges, as these will be used to fold over the finished dish in an envelope effect. Put on another full sheet and brush it with oil.
6. Cut 12 sheets of pastry to fit the base of the dish and put in 5 of them, brushing each layer with oil. Sprinkle the cumin seed evenly over the top layer of pastry and spoon half the watercress cream over it.
7. Lay the filleted fish on top in a single layer, cutting the fillets as necessary to fit them in. Sprinkle with freshly ground black pepper and lemon juice. Spoon the rest of the cream over the fish and smooth the surface.
8. Lay a trimmed sheet of pastry on top, brush it with oil, and continue until you have used up all but one sheet of trimmed pastry, oiling each layer. Now fold over the overhanging pieces of pastry, trimming the corners to get a neat fit. Oil the surface and top with the last piece of pastry. Brush with oil and score the surface in diamond shapes with a sharp knife.
9. Bake for 35-40 minutes until golden on top. Serve cold.

Note:
Filo is a very thin pastry much used in Greece. You will find it in supermarket freezers (labelled filo/strudel pastry) and Greek delicatessen in packets of 400g/14oz which contain about 20 sheets.

Defrost, then carefully unfold to remove the sheets one by one. Keep the pastry covered with a damp towel at all times to make it easily manageable.

In use, filo is always layered with oil or butter to keep the sheets separate. Leftover pastry can be refolded and frozen.

SALAD OF MIXED SUMMER GREENS

For this simply use as many varieties of lettuce as you can find for a colourful effect and good mix of textures. Add fresh herbs such as tarragon, chervil, chives, parsley or coriander.

Make up a vinaigrette using 1 part lemon juice or cider vinegar or one of the fruit vinegars, to 6 parts walnut oil, if you can get it, or extra virgin olive oil. A combination of half and half is good, too. Dress the salad only when you are ready to serve, add seasoning to taste and sprinkle with a few lightly toasted chopped walnuts.

TOMATO AND BASIL SALAD

SERVES 8

500-600g/1-1¼lb firm ripe tomatoes
12 large basil leaves
2 tablespoons extra virgin olive oil
salt and black pepper

1. Slice the tomatoes thinly. Tear the basil leaves into small pieces rather than chop them — they seem to retain their flavour better this way. Sprinkle the basil on the tomatoes and drizzle the oil over both of them. Tomatoes have their own acidity and need no vinegar.
2. Lightly season and allow to stand for at least an hour at room temperature before serving.

SUMMER PUDDING

You can either make one large pudding or eight individual ones — these look extremely pretty, but are rather fiddly. If you don't have dariole moulds, use a set of teacups. The amount of bread you need will depend on the size of the loaf and the cups or pudding basin you use. Two to three smallish slices of bread should be sufficient for one teacup or individual mould.

SERVES 8

medium thin slices of white, wholemeal or Granary bread
500g/1lb raspberries
250g/8oz strawberries, hulled
250g/8oz redcurrants, off the stalk
250g/8oz blackcurrants
50g/2oz sugar
1 cinnamon stick
whipping or pouring cream to serve

1. Trim the crusts from the bread. Cut out a circle for the top of each pudding, then cut the rest into wedge shapes.
2. Pick over the fruit and top and tail the blackcurrants. Put the fruit in a pan with the sugar, cinnamon stick and 2 tablespoons water. Heat gently until the sugar has melted and the fruit has given off a little juice, but don't cook the fruit. Cool the fruit mixture while you fit the bread into the moulds.
3. Remove the cinnamon stick from the pan and divide the fruit equally between the moulds, adding just enough juice to moisten the bread. Keep the rest.
4. Fit the bread 'lids' on top, pour on a little more juice and cover each pudding with foil or cling film. Put weights on top and leave them overnight.
5. To serve, turn the puddings on to serving plates, spoon a puddle of juice round each and trickle a stream of cream over the juice, without stirring.

WINE NOTES

I wonder whether one has to insist on méthode champenoise (*a term that the litigious champagne producers will soon have driven out of use*) *for the sparkling wine that is to be mixed with herbs, fruit and soda? There are some quite adequate* vins mousseux, *made by less laborious and expensive techniques, available at little more than half the price. Look out particularly for the excellent wines from G. F. Cavalier.*

Light, but firm and fruity, summer reds for serving as Frances Bissell suggests are more and more widely available from supermarkets and off-licences, particularly because of the rapid improvement in French vin de pays. *Taste has been in the forefront of breaking down the British prejudice against drinking young red wine chilled (as the French do). We certainly don't object to fruits and sparkling mineral water either, with wines that are intended to be drunk fresh, fruity and young.*

Maddalena Bonino

ITALIAN SUPPER

While not strictly traditional, Maddalena Bonino's light summer menu takes its inspiration from her grandmother's cooking

---

Spaghetti al pomodoro

Trio of fish with hazelnut sauce
Stir-fried carrot ribbons with lime
Herby green salad

Mango and zabaione mousse
Sweet biscuits

From left: spaghetti al pomodoro; stir-fried carrot ribbons with lime; trio of fish with hazelnut sauce; and herby green salad

A quick glance at the menu and the spelling of my name should provide obvious clues as to the Italian connection here. And although this could not be described as a typical Italian meal, most of these recipes are Italian-inspired.

I grew up in northern Italy, with a Piedmontese grandmother and a southern-Italian mother, and was introduced to a great variety of ingredients and spices at a very early age, which made eating always a pleasurable experience. Obviously I'm partial to Italian food, but I also enjoy combining flavours and ingredients from different cuisines.

For this menu I have tried to put together dishes that look and taste delicious, but won't need long and complex preparation. In summer particularly, no one wants to spend hours in a hot kitchen.

Spaghetti is probably my favourite type of pasta, and the best sauces for it are usually very easy to make.

COUNTDOWN

Two days before
• *Make the biscuits to accompany the mousse.*

The day before
• *Make the hazelnut sauce.*

In the morning
• *Skin and fillet the fish.*
• *Make the vinaigrette.*
• *Prepare the salad ingredients and refrigerate them all separately in polythene bags.*

About three hours before
• *Make the mango and zabaione mousse.*

An hour before
• *Make the sauce for the spaghetti.*
• *Prepare the carrot ribbons.*

About 10 minutes before serving
• *Cook the pasta.*
• *Have the steamer ready to cook the fish.*

During the first course
• *Steam the fish.*

After the first course
• *Stir-fry the carrots with lime.*
• *Assemble the green salad.*

Just before serving the dessert
• *Decorate the mousses with whipped cream.*

When cooking a simple dish like this, it's important to choose the ingredients carefully, so buy tomatoes with plenty of flavour and a good brand of spaghetti, such as DeCecco, which can be found in most delicatessen.

If you want to make this a really special dish, try to find the 'ultimate' spaghetti which is produced by Martelli, and available from a few expensive delicatessen in Milan (I also saw it once in Conran).

Fish is particularly suitable for a light summer dinner, and the Middle-Eastern nut sauce that accompanies it adds texture without altering its delicate flavour.

My grandmother taught me how to make zabaione when I was little. She would make it when one of us was feeling off-colour, or hadn't been eating enough, or was convalescing. She firmly believed in its medicinal properties and, sure enough, her zabaione always did the trick. But I'm not sure she'd approve of the way I'm using her recipe here, though!

Good Italian wines are plentiful these days, and the choice available is continually increasing. I asked the writer Mario Soldati, a connoisseur and authority on Italian wines, to suggest what would suit this menu. For the spaghetti he recommends Cerasuolo di Montepulciano d'Abruzzo-Villa Torre, a rosé wine which is fermented without the skins to produce the delicate colour. Or try a Refosco from the Friuli region, preferably not vintage.

With the fish, Mario Soldati suggests a Pinot bianco, from Friuli again, such as Humar or Felluga. And for the dessert Ramandolo di Nimis. The one bottled by Mario Dri is excellent but elusive.

As an aperitif I would serve a light, sparkling wine such as Franciacorta Rosaro Spumante and with it fresh Parmesan, which should be offered in large chunks with a knife for the guests to help themselves.

SPAGHETTI AL POMODORO

SERVES 6

700g/1½lb fresh firm tomatoes
½ garlic clove, finely chopped
5 tablespoons extra virgin olive oil
juice of ½ lemon
12 large basil leaves
salt and freshly ground black pepper
400g/14oz spaghetti
freshly grated Parmesan cheese to serve

1. Blanch the tomatoes, then peel them, remove the seeds and cut them into segments. Set them to marinate in a bowl for about an hour in a cool place with the garlic, oil, lemon juice, half the basil leaves, torn not chopped; season to taste.
2. Cook the spaghetti in salted boiling water for about 10 minutes or until *al dente*. Drain well and toss in the marinade. Serve sprinkled with Parmesan and the remaining basil leaves.

TRIO OF FISH WITH HAZELNUT SAUCE

The choice of fish for this recipe will determine the appearance; I find that the combination of white and pink underlines the lightness of flavour of this dish.

SERVES 6

3 whitings, each about 200-250g/7-8oz
3 pink trout, each about 200-250g/7-8oz
3 red mullets, each about 175-200g/6-7oz
2 tablespoons olive oil
salt
sprigs of dill to garnish
FOR THE HAZELNUT SAUCE
100g/4oz ground hazelnuts
100g/4oz fresh white breadcrumbs
½ garlic clove, chopped
225ml/8fl. oz olive oil
75ml/3fl. oz lemon juice
salt
freshly ground black pepper

1. Fillet and skin the whitings and the trout; remove the scales and fillet the red mullets (or ask the fishmonger to do it for you). Use a pair of tweezers to ensure that all the bones have been removed. Cut the fillets of whiting, trout and red mullet diagonally so that all the pieces of fish are of a similar size.
2. Heat the water in the base of a steamer to simmering point. Put the fish in batches into the steamer and cover tightly. Steam for about 8-10 minutes or until the fish is just firm to the touch. Keep it warm, covered with foil, in a low oven until you are ready to serve it. Alternatively, if you do not have a steamer, you can steam the fish in batches sandwiched between 2 plates and placed over a pan of boiling water until tender.
3. Put the hazelnuts, breadcrumbs and chopped garlic in a blender. With the machine running, add the oil slowly but steadily, then the lemon juice and 200ml/7fl. oz of water. Season to taste. Pour into a bowl, cover and leave in the refrigerator until the sauce is needed.
4. Now arrange the fish on a large warmed platter or on individual plates. Drizzle the olive oil over them and sprinkle with a little salt if necessary. Garnish the fish with sprigs of dill, and serve with the bowl of hazelnut sauce.

STIR-FRIED CARROT RIBBONS WITH LIME

SERVES 6

700g/1½lb carrots
3 tablespoons oil
salt and freshly ground black pepper
grated zest of 2 limes
juice of 1 lime

1. Peel the carrots, to remove outer skin, then keep 'peeling' the carrots to obtain ribbons (discard the hard white central core). Heat the oil and stir-fry the ribbons for a few minutes — the carrots should be crunchy — then season to taste and serve sprinkled with the grated lime zest and lime juice.

HERBY GREEN SALAD WITH LIME VINAIGRETTE

SERVES 6

a selection of green leaves: cos lettuce, endive, chicory, lamb's lettuce, watercress
2-3 sprigs fresh mint
2-3 sprigs fresh dill
FOR THE VINAIGRETTE
4 tablespoons olive oil
½ teaspoon salt
½ teaspoon dry mustard
½ teaspoon clear honey
juice of 1 lime

1. Wash and dry the salad leaves, and tear them into bite-sized pieces.
2. Put the ingredients for the vinaigrette in a screw-top jar and shake well. Check seasoning. Toss the salad with the lime vinaigrette dressing and sprinkle with whole mint leaves and the roughly chopped dill.

MANGO AND ZABAIONE MOUSSE

SERVES 6

FOR THE MANGO MOUSSE
½ teaspoon gelatine
50ml/2fl. oz double cream
2 egg whites
300ml/½pt mango purée
orange food colouring (optional)
FOR THE ZABAIONE
3 egg yolks
3 tablespoons caster sugar
3 tablespoons white wine
4 tablespoons Marsala wine
50ml/2fl. oz double cream
1 egg white
50ml/2fl. oz double cream, whipped, for decoration (optional)

1. Halve all the quantities for the mango mousse and proceed as follows. Soak the gelatine in ½ tablespoon water. Whip the double cream until it holds its shape but is not too stiff. Whisk the egg white until stiff but not dry. Dissolve the gelatine and pour it into the mango

purée, stirring well; add food colouring if liked. Fold in the whipped cream, then the egg white.
2. Divide the mixture between 6 glasses (250ml/9fl. oz capacity) and leave to set in the refrigerator, on a slant, for about 40 minutes. (Use a bed of crumpled foil in a tray to support the slanted glasses.) While the mango mousse sets make the zabaione.
3. Put the yolks and sugar in a bowl or the top pan of a double boiler and whisk well. Place the bowl over, but not touching, gently simmering water, add the wine and the Marsala, and keep whisking until the mixture has thickened and is light and fluffy. Remove from the heat and leave to cool, whisking occasionally.
4. In separate bowls, whisk the cream until it holds its shape and the egg white until stiff; then fold first the cream, then the egg white, into the cooled zabaione. Pour a layer of this on top of the mango mousse in the glasses and return to the refrigerator for at least another 40 minutes.
5. Make the mango mousse as before, and when the zabaione is set, top up the glasses with it. Keep in the refrigerator until required. Serve decorated with whipped cream and home-made biscuits.

COCONUT TUILES

MAKES ABOUT 18

1 egg white
50g/2oz caster sugar
25g/1oz melted unsalted butter, cooled, plus extra for greasing
25g/1oz sifted flour, plus extra for dusting
3 tablespoons desiccated coconut

1. Heat the oven to 190C/375F/gas 5. Whisk the egg white until stiff, add the caster sugar and keep whisking until very stiff. Fold in the melted butter, then the flour and the coconut.
2. Using a circular motion, spread small amounts of the mixture on to greased and floured baking trays to

form circles measuring about 8cm/3in. Bake in batches for 5-6 minutes, until golden. Remove from the baking tray, place over a rolling pin, and leave to cool and become crisp. Store in an airtight container.

Note:

When shaping the biscuits work quickly as the biscuits become crisp the moment they cool. If they harden too soon, it is possible to soften them again by popping them back in the oven for a few seconds, before shaping them on the rolling pin.

VANILLA TWISTS

MAKES ABOUT 16

100g/4oz flour, plus extra for dusting
50g/2oz icing sugar
75g/3oz cold unsalted butter, cubed, plus extra for greasing
vanilla essence
1 small egg yolk, beaten

1. Sift the flour on to a work surface and make a well in the centre. Sift the icing sugar into it and make another well in the centre. Put the cubed butter in the well and work it with your fingertips until soft, drawing in a little sugar at a time.

2. When the butter and sugar are mixed, add a few drops of vanilla essence and start incorporating the flour. Add enough egg yolk to bind the mixture together — the dough should be soft but not sticky. Roll the pastry into a ball, cover and leave to rest in a cool place for 30 minutes.

3. Heat the oven to 190C/375F/gas 5. Grease 2 baking trays and dust lightly with flour.

4. Using a little dough at a time, roll out on a lightly floured surface to form a fairly thin 'sausage', cut into lengths of about 15cm/6in, fold in half and twist. Place the biscuits well apart on the baking trays. Bake for 8-10 minutes, until golden in colour. Remove from the oven, leave to cool completely and then store in an airtight container.

CORNMEAL BISCUITS

MAKES ABOUT 16

50g/2oz cornmeal flour (also known as polenta or maize flour)
25g/1oz plain flour, plus extra
50g/2oz unsalted butter at room temperature, cubed, plus extra for greasing
25g/1oz caster sugar
grated zest of ½ orange
1 small egg yolk

1. Sift the cornmeal and plain flour on to a work surface, and make a well in the centre. Place the cubed butter and sugar in the well and work them together with your fingertips until well mixed. Add the orange zest and yolk. Keep working with your fingertips, drawing in all the flour.

2. Form the dough into a ball, cover and leave to rest for 30 minutes in a cool place. Heat the oven to 200C/400F/ gas 6.

3. Roll out the pastry on to a lightly floured surface until fairly thin, then with a biscuit-cutter cut out the biscuits. Place the biscuits on greased and floured baking trays and bake for 6-8 minutes, until golden.

WINE NOTES

As befits an Italian wine expert, Mario Soldati has provided a counsel of perfection in his choice of wines – but precisely because fine Italian wines are so well appreciated by Italians they are difficult to find here. One of the best lists to consult is that of Winecellars (01-871-2668), where Italian wine enthusiasts and Masters of Wine Nicholas Belfrage and David Gleave gather much that is classiest from Italy. It was Belfrage who wrote the aptly titled introduction to good Italian wine – Life Beyond Lambrusco. Their selection is likely to include a classic, bright and fresh Cerasuolo. If you go for it, serve it chilled for fruitiest effect. Other Italians that would bring an appropriately light touch include Bardolino. Supermarket shoppers should look out for Italian reds and pinks with style indicators A or B – like light, clean and sweetly simple Valdadige Rosso or decent Refosco. Alternatives for the fish would include Vernaccia di San Gimignano or aromatic Bianco di Custoza. Among finer Italian whites, elusive Fiano d'Avellino has built its high reputation and price on its affinity with hazelnuts, so enthusiasts might want to hunt that down. Stick, in any case, with the supermarket-style indicators 1 or 2. The delicious Ramondolo, which is occasionally available from Italian specialist wine suppliers, will round things out sweetly at the end, if you can find it.

Suzy Benghiat

SUMMER BARBECUE PARTY

Middle-Eastern-style food is ideal for outdoor cooking and large gatherings, so consult the weather forecast and light the fire, says Suzy Benghiat

Egyptian salad
Tabbouleh
Tahina and yoghurt dips

Aubergine purée
Sweet pepper salad
Barbecued fish
Koftas
Lamb cutlets
Poussins

Grilled Halumi cheese
Fresh fruit, watermelon and Feta cheese

Since kebabs of all sorts have become standard barbecue fare in this country, and as kebabs originated in the Middle East, it is generally assumed that barbecue parties have always been a general practice there. I am often asked about memories of the barbecues of my childhood in Egypt. I'm afraid I don't have any!

Unless you count the picnics our group used to organize by a derelict water reservoir in a Cairo suburb. The boys would try to impress us with the skills they had acquired as Boy Scouts, and insisted that we should cook on an open fire. When, after several smoky attempts and lots of puffing and swearing, they succeeded in getting it going, they would take out an old frying pan and empty into it the contents of a huge tin of baked beans to warm up. Luckily, we could get excellent *foul* and *falafel* sandwiches (made from beans and rissoles) nearby!

Nevertheless, charcoal cooking does evoke sensuous memories. When turning a corner we would smell the most enticing smoke, fragrant with the combined aromas of charred lamb, garlic, onion and spices emanating from a specialist restaurant or kiosk selling kebabs and koftas, accompanied by salads and pickles, to go with warm Arabic bread.

Driving to the Pyramids for some fresh, cool desert air on a warm summer evening, we would stop the car to buy some young golden corn cobs roasting over gently burning embers, nonchalantly fanned by a

Middle Eastern mezze, *including a selection of crudités, pickles, olives, salads and dips, pitta bread and crunchy sesame sticks*

COUNTDOWN

Three hours before
- *Trim lamb cutlets and leave to marinate.*
- *Prepare poussins, and marinate.*
- *Make yoghurt and tahina dips (do not garnish tahina dip with cumin seeds yet), and refrigerate until needed.*

Two hours before
- *Mix ingredients for lamb, and lamb and beef koftas, and shape. Cover with cling film and leave in a cool place (preferably not the refrigerator).*
- *Prepare sea bass and/or monkfish, if using, coat with paste and leave, covered, in the refrigerator.*
- *Wash, gut and dry sardines, if using.*
- *Wash, de-vein and dry king prawns, if using.*
- *Chill white wine.*

One hour before
- *Remove fish from the refrigerator and put in a cool place.*
- *Make tabbouleh and leave, covered, in a cool place.*
- *Open red wine.*

Half an hour before
- *Make Eygptian salad.*
- *Make dressings for sardines and king prawns, if using.*
- *Dip sardines, if using, in bran.*
- *Thin tahina paste if necessary and garnish with cumin seeds.*

dozing vendor. While nibbling greedily at the sweet kernels, we would inhale the perfume of the jasmine necklaces bought from the intrepid traffic dodgers, who used to jump deftly on to passing cars as they slowed down.

But I am sure that the barbecue fashion that has come to us from the United States has also hit the Middle East. I can imagine beach and desert parties when the smart westernized set show off their brand-new electric barbecues, on which they cook hamburgers, to be served up with tomato ketchup and American relishes poured straight from a bottle.

However, it is true that Middle Eastern food and customs are ideally suited to a barbecue. You can easily organize your own in an English garden or patio, even at short notice. But for this, and in order that everyone enjoys the experience of participating, it is vital to plan ahead. Organize helpers; some of them will opt for making their favourite salads, while others will take on the marinating. Guests who live near a specialist shop or market can bring the bread, pickles, cheeses and olives that will be part of the *mezze* spread of traditional hors d'oeuvre dishes, always laid out ready on the table, to keep hunger at bay while waiting for the barbecued food to cook.

Mezze are similar to Spanish tapas or Italian antipasto, and can even be a meal in themselves if they are varied enough. For simplicity choose a selection of crudités, pickles, olives and small cubes of cheese, a couple of salads and dips with lots of bread such as Arabic, pitta and crunchy sesame sticks.

For the crudités, you will need three or four cos lettuces with the outer leaves removed. Cut the lettuces in half lengthways, and arrange them at one end of a large oval dish. Trim a couple of bunches of radishes, leaving a little of the

green top on for its peppery flavour. Halve or quarter a dozen Mediterranean cucumbers. (This variety is about the length of a ridge cucumber but they have a smooth skin. Don't confuse them with similar-looking cucumbers from Holland, which are watery and tasteless.) Add a couple of bunches of trimmed spring onions.

A selection of olives could include Greek, Italian and Spanish black olives, and perhaps some green olives with coriander and chilli from Egypt. I buy olives loose wherever possible, because they are cheaper that way.

Polish cucumbers in brine are delicious, and Indian pickles from Asian grocers are good, too. But my favourites are pink turnips from the Lebanon or Egypt; the inclusion of a beetroot in the pickling jar transforms turnips to a fuchsia pink.

Once the fire is lit, start on the aubergine purée and sweet pepper salad. Vegetables are cooked first, as soon as the flames have receded. When the cinders have turned grey and you have hot charcoal, the main course can be barbecued. Fish takes just a few minutes, so it is cooked and eaten before meat and poultry. Choose one or more of the following suggestions according to the number of people and the importance of the occasion: fish; meat; poultry; sausages. The main course will be marinated and flavoured with the characteristic herbs and spices of the Middle East: cumin; coriander; mint; parsley; onion; garlic; chilli; dill; rosemary. According to taste, you can eat the barbecued food with some of the dips, salads and pickles from the mezze spread. Barbecued slices of Halumi cheese are really delicious because they absorb all the flavours of the meats cooked before them.

For dessert, choose the fresh ripe fruits in season like grapes, dates, figs, plums, apricots and peaches. Cut a peeled watermelon into wedges or chunks for eating with fingers or cocktail sticks, and serve it with small cubes of Feta cheese, a delicious combination of colours, flavours and textures. Feta cheese also goes well with grapes.

All that is needed now is warm sunshine with a very slight breeze to bring out the fragrance of your summer flowers. Even if the weather lets you down, you can always transfer everything indoors and do your grilling in the kitchen, some items under the grill and some on top of the stove, using metal grids or heat diffusers.

To complete the illusion — exotic for some, nostalgic for others — set bowls of white jasmine (it grows well in British gardens) or vases of freesias around the room.

EGYPTIAN SALAD

Roughly chop a mixture of firm tomatoes, cucumbers and spring onions. Add a finely chopped garlic clove and chopped flat-leaved parsley. Mix well and add salt, lemon or lime juice to taste, some olive oil and ground cumin.

TABBOULEH

SERVES 6-8
1 cup dry burghul
2-3 handfuls finely chopped flat-leaved parsley
1 handful mint, finely chopped
1 handful fresh coriander, chopped
2 small cucumbers, chopped
4-5 spring onions, including green part, roughly chopped
juice of 2 lemons or limes
olive or sunflower oil
salt

1. Soak burghul for 10-15 minutes. Strain it through muslin and squeeze all the moisture out. Place in a large bowl with all the other ingredients except oil; mix well, then add some oil and mix again. Taste and season with salt.

TAHINA DIP

SERVES 6-8
1 jar tahina paste
2 garlic cloves
salt
juice of 2 lemons
⅓ teaspoon ground cumin

1. Stir the contents of the jar thoroughly to blend the paste. Crush the garlic with a little salt. Mix about 2 tablespoons of the tahina paste with the garlic in a large mixing bowl. Add the rest of the tahina and mix well.
2. Add about 1 tablespoon lemon juice and stir, then gradually add water (2 tablespoons at a time). The mixture will thicken and seem to separate — do not be alarmed. At this stage, taste, adding more salt and lemon juice if necessary.
3. Continue adding water, then add the juice of half a lemon. Stir vigorously after each addition until you obtain a smooth thick texture like mayonnaise. Taste again and, if you like a more tangy flavour, add more lemon juice.
4. Transfer into small bowls and sprinkle the cumin over the top. If the mixture thickens up, add a little water and give it a good stir.

YOGHURT DIP

Mix 1 large carton plain Greek yoghurt, 1 tablespoon dried crushed mint, some grated onion, a pinch of chilli powder and salt. Stir well, taste and adjust seasoning if necessary.

AUBERGINE PURÉE

SERVES 6-8
3 aubergines
2 garlic cloves
salt and pepper
juice of 1 lemon
1-2 tablespoons olive oil
chopped flat-leaved parsley

1. Wash and dry the aubergines and place them on a grid over the fire,

turning them from time to time. When the skin starts to burst, the flesh will be soft and cooked. Skin the aubergines and chop the pulp finely.
2. Crush the garlic with a little salt, then add freshly ground pepper and lemon juice. Mix well with the purée then add the oil; taste and adjust seasoning if necessary. Serve in a bowl with the parsley sprinkled on top.

SWEET PEPPER SALAD

SERVES 6
2-3 large green peppers
2-3 large yellow peppers
2-3 large red peppers
2-3 garlic cloves
sea salt
white malt vinegar
olive or sunflower oil

1. Cook the peppers by placing them on a grid over the fire, turning them from time to time, until the skins blister. Put the peppers in a large bowl and place it inside a plastic bag; after 10 minutes in the steamy bag, the peppers will be easy to peel.
2. Remove the seeds; dry the peppers on absorbent paper and dice them. Mix the colours together or season them separately: chop the garlic very finely and sprinkle it over the peppers; add salt and dribble over some vinegar.
3. Leave the peppers for 10 minutes, then mix together and add oil. Taste and adjust seasoning if necessary.

Note:
Don't bother to buy the purplish-black peppers from Holland, because they revert to green as they are cooked.

BARBECUED FISH

Buy fish as fresh as possible. Small fish like sardines, herring and mackerel can be cooked whole; sea bass, grey mullet and monkfish can be barbecued in slices. Grilled king-size prawns are a very special treat.

FRESH SARDINES

Wash under running cold water; remove the head and guts by twisting the head and pulling. Dry the fish on absorbent paper and dip them in bran. Place the fish on the grid over the fire and cook for 1-2 minutes, then turn and cook the other side. Transfer the fish to a plate and pour over a dressing made from 1 part lemon juice, 2 parts water, seasoned with salt and pepper to taste.

KING-SIZE PRAWNS

Wash and de-vein the raw prawns and pat dry on absorbent paper; cook on a grid over the fire until they turn pink. Dress with the mixture given above for sardines.

SEA BASS

Ask the fishmonger to scale the fish and cut into 1cm/½in slices. Discard the head and tail: this means that you will find it easier to remove the guts from the centre of the slices, keeping the slices in shape.

Wash and dry the slices. Coat them with a paste made from equal quantities of crushed garlic, ground cumin and chopped flat-leaved parsley, combined with olive or sunflower oil. Grill on both sides over the fire.

MONKFISH

Trim, then slice as for sea bass. Coat the fish slices with a paste made from equal quantities of crushed garlic, ground cumin, chopped flat-leaved parsley, lemon juice and olive and sunflower oil. Grill the slices on both sides over the fire.

LAMB KOFTA

MAKES 10 KOFTAS

500g/1lb minced lamb

1 onion, finely chopped

½ teaspoon ground cumin

1 tablespoon finely chopped flat-leaved parsley

salt and pepper

1. Mix all the ingredients together and knead into small flat cakes or sausage shapes. Grill the koftas on both sides.

LAMB AND BEEF KOFTA

MAKES 10 KOFTAS

250g/8oz minced lamb

250g/8oz minced beef

1 onion, finely chopped

½ teaspoon ground cumin

1 tablespoon finely chopped flat-leaved parsley

½ teaspoon turmeric

½ teaspoon cinnamon

chilli powder or sauce, to taste

1. Mix all the ingredients thoroughly, and then shape them into small sausage shapes. Grill the koftas on all sides.

LAMB CUTLETS

Trim away all the fat except round the bone from best end of neck chops. Marinate them in a mixture of grated onion, lemon juice and salt and pepper, for several hours. Remove from the marinade and grill them on both sides over the fire.

POUSSINS

Split the birds in half; separate the legs and flatten all the pieces with a meat mallet. Marinate for several hours in the following mixture: thin slivers of garlic; shavings of fresh ginger; a piece of chilli; lemon juice; olive oil; salt and pepper. Cook over the fire, turning the pieces often to ensure even cooking.

GRILLED HALUMI CHEESE

This cooking cheese is available from Greek and Cypriot grocers and delicatessen.

Simply grill the slices on the grid for a minute or two each side. Don't worry, it won't melt.

Above: meat, poultry and sausages;
Right: dessert of watermelon and Feta

WINE NOTES

Usually I like to recommend wines with a regional association with the food they are to accompany, but I am afraid the idea threatens to fall down when we get to the Middle East. Most of the wines are not good enough to offer much tasting excitement.

The Moroccan wines, Tarik and Sidi Larbi, are sound but rather rough and ready. Similarly Buzbag from Turkey is too fiery, even for a barbecue.

There is now some young and generous Cabernet Sauvignon from a modern Israeli winery on the Golan Heights under the Gamla label, so that has to be it, apart from Lebanon's excellent Château Musar, if the red wine is to come from the Middle East. Israel has a possible white, too, in Yarden (it means Jordan) Sauvignon, a good pungent and fresh varietal.

But you may find it easier to go for two multi-purpose wines that will please everyone with a mixed barbecue. For white, a good crisp Sauvignon is ideal as an appetizing aperitif, and fruity enough to cope with crudités. For red, the safest bet is likely to be one of the much improved French vin de pays or an evocatively spice-and-cedar-scented red from the southern Rhône; or an Australian red featuring the Rhône's classic grape (known down under as Shiraz) – the sort of wine Australians fuel their barbies with, no doubt. You can serve many of them cool, too, to quench the fires of your thirst.

Antony Kwok

ORIENTAL DINNER FOR A SUMMER EVENING

*Prolong the pleasure of a warm August night with
Antony Kwok's light and delicate dinner*

Summer garden vegetables in filo nests

Iced salad of seafood and noodles with sesame sauce

Hot spicy lamb with bamboo shoots and a mélange of mushrooms

Steamed coriander buns

Jasmine tea sorbet

If there is one thing that I enjoy as much as cooking, it is shopping for food. This has become much easier in the last few years, with supermarkets offering a much wider choice of produce than ever before. When I first arrived in London from Hong Kong, in the early 1970s, avocados were still considered exotic and were not widely on sale. Anything slightly unusual had to be sought in shops serving the various ethnic communities of London.

In planning this menu, I have drawn inspiration from different parts of the Orient, but with a strong Chinese emphasis. Traditionally, there are no courses in Chinese family meals; all the dishes are served simultaneously. The meal is

COUNTDOWN

The day before

• *Make the lamb stock and chill.*
• *Make the dough for the coriander buns. Shape the buns, then wrap and chill them.*
• *Make the sorbet.*
• *Make the ice bowl for the noodles.*

On the day

• *Boil the noodles; drain and chill them.*
• *Marinate the prawns and arrange all the seafood salad ingredients on a serving plate. Cover with cling film and chill.*
• *Make the vinaigrette and the sesame sauce.*
• *Make the filo nests and store in a tissue-lined tin.*

Six hours before serving

• *Take the buns out of the refrigerator and bring to room temperature.*
• *Infuse the wine and five spices.*

One hour before serving

• *Soak the dried mushrooms in cold water.*
• *Strain the spiced wine.*
• *Salt and drain the bitter gourd.*

Just before serving

• *Season the lamb with the spiced wine.*
• *Slice the bamboo shoots.*
• *Warm the filo nests in the oven and stir-fry the filling; serve with the aperitifs.*

Just before the first course

• *Toss the salad leaves in the vinaigrette and arrange on the serving platter with the other seafood salad ingredients.*

After the first course

• *Cook the lamb and mushrooms.*
• *Soften the sorbet in the refrigerator.*

often finished with fresh fruit rather than a dessert; sweet dishes are treated more as snacks. In a formal banquet, however, dishes are usually served in a succession of nine or more courses, with a soup course in the middle of the meal.

This menu is designed as four courses, and with carefully planned shopping and advance preparation, it should not present too many problems on the day. I often use dinner parties as an excuse to be a bit more extravagant than usual when buying ingredients. Although friends often drop by to share a wok-ful of stir-fried vegetables and rice or pasta during the week, it is rewarding to make the extra effort, especially at weekends. For this meal, a warm summer's night is excuse enough.

Because I am a firm believer in using good home-made stock as a basis, I ask the butcher to prepare the meat as required and collect it in the middle of the week. The bones and trimmings are turned into stock, which is stored in the refrigerator. The spices used to flavour the lamb are known collectively in China as the five fragrances, and are originally the speciality of Western (Sichuan) cuisine.

The salad leaves and herbs can also be purchased in advance. Remove any tough or bruised parts; soak the whole plants in cold water with ice cubes for 30 to 60 minutes to refresh, then shake off most of the water and store in the refrigerator, loosely wrapped in plastic bags.

One aperitif that would start off the meal is a champagne cocktail — one of my concoctions is based on kumquats soaked in Grand Marnier. A crisp dry white wine such as a Chablis would go well with the iced noodle salad, but only a full-bodied red wine will stand up to the spices in the main course. To round off the meal, I would serve crystallized ginger and cinnamon-flavoured tuiles with coffee.

SUMMER GARDEN VEGETABLES IN FILO NESTS

These little canapés set the scene for the meal. The nests can be made in advance, to be reheated and filled just before serving. For the filling choose at least three different vegetables to give contrast in colour and texture, for example sweet red pepper with baby sweetcorn and artichoke hearts or asparagus with *daikon* (mooli) and fennel or celery.

MAKES 12 NESTS

1 teaspoon light soy sauce
1 teaspoon dry sherry
3 teaspoons vegetable oil
100g/4oz chicken breast, finely chopped
1 garlic clove, finely chopped
1 small piece ginger, finely chopped
150g/5oz mixed vegetables, finely diced
lemon juice to taste
salt and freshly ground pepper
FOR THE NESTS
4 sheets of ready-made filo pastry, trimmed and cut into 48×7.5cm/3in squares
40g/1½oz melted butter, plus extra for greasing
FOR THE GARNISH
3 quail eggs, hard-boiled and shelled
6 sprigs chervil
6 slender asparagus tips
6 baby sweetcorn, tips only

1. Make the filo nests. Heat the oven to 180C/350F/gas 4. Keep the pastry covered with a damp cloth to prevent it from drying out. Assemble each nest from 4 squares, brushed generously with melted butter. Place one square on top of another, turning each successive square through a few degrees so that you end up with a star with 16 points.
2. Brush both sides of the stars with more melted butter and press into small tartlet moulds. Open out a little to make the points stand out. Line with grease-proof paper and baking beans and bake

ICED SALAD OF SEAFOOD AND NOODLES WITH SESAME SAUCE

This is an adaptation of a northern Chinese dish which has long been popular in Peking during the unbearably hot summer months. The Japanese have a similar version for the same reason. Because I like to mix and serve the salad at table, everything can be prepared beforehand, garnished and kept in the refrigerator. I have used Japanese *sansho* pepper to add a subtle perfume to the sauce.

SERVES 6

75g/3oz dried noodles
1½ tablespoons sesame oil
175g/6oz whole prawns, shelled (use the roe, too, if available)
2 tablespoons dry white wine
100g/4oz smoked salmon
100g/4oz smoked tofu or 175g/6oz fresh tofu, pressed and drained for 2 hours over a cloth-lined sieve
½ cucumber, peeled and cut into julienne strips
100g/4oz beansprouts or shredded Chinese leaves
10g/⅓oz dry wakame seaweed, soaked in cold water for 30 minutes, drained and squeezed dry
a selection of salad leaves including red-leaved lettuce, Batavia endive, frisée, lamb's lettuce, mustard and cress, and watercress
golden caviar (salmon roe) or red lumpfish roe and toasted sesame seeds to garnish
FOR THE SESAME SAUCE
125ml/4fl. oz sesame oil
3 tablespoons white wine vinegar
3 tablespoons tahina
1 teaspoon mustard powder
1 teaspoon soy sauce
1 teaspoon nam pla (Thai fish sauce)
½ tablespoon sansho pepper
salt and cayenne pepper
FOR THE VINAIGRETTE
2 tablespoons sesame oil
1 teaspoon lemon juice
salt and freshly ground pepper

for 5-10 minutes. Remove the nests from the tins, turn upside down and cook for a further 3-4 minutes until golden and crisp.

3. Remove the nests from the oven and cool on a wire rack. If making in advance, store them in a tissue-lined container.

4. Mix the soy sauce, sherry and a teaspoon of the oil in a bowl. Toss in the chicken and marinate for 10-15 minutes.

5. Prepare the garnish. Cut the quail eggs in half and garnish each half with a sprig of chervil. Blanch the asparagus tips and the tips of the baby sweetcorn. Refresh in cold water and drain.

6. Heat the remaining vegetable oil in a wok until just smoking. Toss in the garlic and ginger. Stir for half a minute. Add the crunchier vegetables (e.g. celery, fennel), then the chicken, stirring constantly until the meat begins to turn white. Add the other vegetables, a squeeze of lemon juice and stir-fry for another minute. Remove from the heat and season.

7. Reheat the filo nests in the oven for 3-5 minutes. Spoon the hot chicken salad into the nests, garnish some with quail egg halves and some with the asparagus and baby sweetcorn tips. Serve with the aperitif.

1. Cook the noodles in salted water with a tablespoon of oil, until *al dente*. Refresh in cold water. Drain, put in a serving bowl and cover with cling film; chill until needed.

2. Marinate the prawns and their roe in the white wine and remaining ½ tablespoon of oil for 30 minutes. Drain the prawns.

3. Cut the smoked salmon and tofu into thin strips. Arrange the prawns, smoked salmon, tofu, cucumber, beansprouts, and seaweed attractively in the centre of a platter. Cover and chill.

4. Mix the sesame sauce ingredients together; taste and season. Wash and drain the salad leaves. Tear into bite-size pieces, place them in a bowl, cover and chill. Make a vinaigrette with the sesame oil and lemon juice, and add seasoning.

5. Toss the salad leaves with the vinaigrette and arrange on the platter. To serve at table, toss the noodles with the vegetables, tofu, seaweed and sesame sauce. Serve each guest some salad leaves and place a twirl of noodles in the centre. Top with the salmon or lumpfish roe and sesame seeds.

Note:

Make an ice bowl to serve the noodles in. Place a glass bowl on a bed of crushed ice inside a bigger bowl (at least 2.5cm/1in wider all round). Fill the space between the two bowls with more crushed ice and iced water. Weigh down the inner bowl if necessary, without letting the water overflow into it. Freeze for at least 24 hours before use. To unmould, dip the outside bowl very briefly in hot water.

HOT SPICY LAMB WITH BAMBOO SHOOTS AND A MÉLANGE OF MUSHROOMS

Some fresh mushrooms such as oyster, *champignons marrons*, *shiitake* or *chanterelles* should be included in the mélange. Dried mushrooms should also be included for their stronger flavour, for example morels, horn of plenty, Italian *porcini* and Chinese black fungus (wood ears).

SERVES 6

2 star anise
2 pieces of cinnamon
1 teaspoon Sichuan pepper
1 teaspoon fennel seed
4 cloves
a few dried chillies (optional)
175ml/6fl. oz dry red wine
175g/6oz mixed fresh mushrooms, sliced
75g/3oz mixed dried mushrooms
1 average loin of lamb, about 1kg/2lb, boned out to give 250-275g/8-9oz eye of loin without fat
salt and freshly ground pepper
25g/1oz butter
4 shallots, finely chopped
1 garlic clove, crushed
small piece fresh ginger, finely grated
250g/8oz bamboo shoots (fresh or canned), thinly sliced
FOR THE STOCK
bones from the loin, trimmed of fat
1 marrow bone, weighing 500g/1lb
1 onion, unpeeled, studded with 2 cloves
50g/2oz Florence fennel, chopped
1 leek, white part only, sliced
mushroom trimmings
1 carrot, cut into chunks
2 garlic cloves, unpeeled
FOR THE GARNISH
1 bitter gourd or melon, sliced and seeded (or canned)
25g/1oz butter
150ml/¼pt apple juice
pinch of salt
1 tablespoon sugar
1 red chilli, seeded and sliced into rings

1. Make the stock. Put the bones and vegetables in a roasting tin and brown in the oven heated to 225-240C/425-475F/gas 7-9, turning constantly to prevent burning. Remove the vegetables and bones after about 20-40 minutes and place in a large stock pot. Pour away the fat from the roasting tin; deglaze the tin with hot water and add to the stock pot. Add enough water to cover. Bring to the boil, then simmer for 4 hours, skimming occasionally. Strain. Let the stock cool, then skim off the fat. Boil to reduce to a syrupy consistency.

2. Add the five spices with the dried chillies, if used, to the red wine. Simmer for 5 minutes; cover and leave to cool and macerate for at least 4 hours, then remove the chillies. Soak the dried mushrooms in cold water for at least 1 hour. After they have plumped up, strain and reserve 300ml/½pt of soaking liquid. Remove and discard tough stalks from the mushrooms. Slice the caps.

3. Cut the lamb into large matchsticks. Season with salt and pepper and 2 tablespoons of the strained spiced red wine, and leave for no longer than 30 minutes.

4. For the garnish, sprinkle the bitter gourd with salt and drain in a colander for 30 minutes. Rinse well and pat dry. Fry lightly in a little butter for 1 minute on each side. Add the apple juice, sugar and salt, and boil for 5 minutes to glaze. Drain and keep warm.

5. Lightly brown the lamb in half the butter. Remove and keep warm. Add the rest of the butter and fry the fresh mushrooms for 2-3 minutes. Remove and keep warm. Fry the shallots, garlic and ginger for 1 minute. Add the dried mushrooms and fry for another minute.

6. Pour in the mushrooms' soaking liquid and simmer for 10 minutes to reduce by half. Add 300ml/½pt of stock and the spiced wine; boil until thick and syrupy. Add the fresh mushrooms and bamboo shoots. Simmer for 5 minutes. Add the lamb and heat through.

7. To serve, place a ring of bitter gourd on each plate and pile with lamb, mushrooms and bamboo shoots: sprinkle on red chilli. Spoon some sauce over and serve with the steamed coriander buns.

Note:
Bitter gourd, the balsam pear, and its relation the balsam apple, is much used in Chinese and Indian dishes. You can buy it canned, occasionally fresh, from Oriental stores.

STEAMED CORIANDER BUNS

MAKES 12

15g/½oz fresh yeast or 1½ teaspoons dried yeast
½ teaspoon sugar
150ml/¼pt warm water
500g/1lb strong white flour, plus extra for dusting
1 teaspoon salt
oil for greasing
1 tablespoon chopped spring onion, white part only
2 tablespoons roughly chopped coriander leaves
coriander leaves, to garnish

1. Add the yeast and sugar to the warm water. Mix well and leave in a warm place for about 10 minutes until foamy. Sieve the flour and salt into the mixing bowl; make a well in the centre and pour in the yeast mixture. Mix well until the mixture leaves the sides of the bowl clean. Knead well on a floured surface until elastic, adding a little more water if necessary.

2. Place the dough in an oiled bowl, cover with oiled cling film and leave in a warm place to rise for about 2 hours, until it has doubled in volume.

3. Divide the dough in 2 — keep half for future use. Roll out one half into a rectangle 15 × 24cm/6 × 9in. Sprinkle with the spring onion and chopped coriander. Roll up along the long edge like a Swiss roll; brush with water to seal and cut into 6 pieces. Place on squares of oiled greaseproof paper. (If preparing the buns in advance, wrap and chill. Bring to room temperature for 4-6 hours before steaming.) Leave the buns to rise in a warm place for about 30 minutes.

4. Steam the buns in batches in a steamer, or in a sieve or colander over a pan of water, covered with a lid. Steam over high heat for 20 minutes. To serve, peel off the paper and garnish each bun with coriander leaves.

WINE NOTES

Those who want an elegant, aromatic and grapey white wine instead of a cocktail are recommended to try the current vintage of the white Pamela Branco dry Muscat by João Pires & Filhos of Portugal. Successive vintages have been received with rapture and excitement.

I have gone off Chablis, though. Its price rises have tended to outstrip its quality, and there are now better Chardonnay values to be had from Italy, Chile, New Zealand, California and, of course, Australia.

The last-named can do full-bodied red at good prices too. Penfolds and Hardys are among the most dependable producers.

For a dessert wine, I would take a Sauternes or similar French sweetie, to be sipped after, rather than with, the sorbet.

JASMINE TEA SORBET

SERVES 6

15g/½oz jasmine tea
450ml/¾pt boiling water
100g/4oz sugar
150ml/¼pt iced water
juice of 1 lemon
2 egg whites
few drops jasmine essence (optional)
6 sprigs mint, frosted with sugar, plus frosted jasmine blossom, to garnish

1. Warm a bowl by rinsing it with hot water. Put in the tea leaves, pour over the boiling water and cover the bowl. Leave to infuse for 5-7 minutes. Strain the tea. Pick out the petals and put them back into the liquid. Transfer to a saucepan, add the sugar and stir over a low heat until dissolved.

2. Pour the liquid into a container. Add the iced water and lemon juice and stir well. Freeze for 2 hours or until the mixture is slushy. Beat the mixture or use a food processor, but chill the bowl first. Whisk the egg whites until stiff and fold into the iced mixture.

3. Freeze for 1½ hours and break up the ice as before. Repeat at least once.

4. Move the sorbet from the freezer to the refrigerator 15 minutes before serving. Serve in chilled wine goblets and garnish with frosted mint and blossom.

Note:

If you can get hold of some Thai edible jasmine essence (*yod nam malee*) add it with the egg whites. If not, try this trick: rub a few drops of jasmine perfume or essential oil on the outside of the glass to release the scent of jasmine when eating the sorbet.

Frances Bissell

LATE SUMMER DINNER

Bid farewell to the summer with an extravagant last fling — Frances Bissell's exquisite menu fits the bill perfectly

---

Parcels of pasta with scallops and saffron sauce

Breasts of chicken with dill and lemon gin sauce
Carrot purée
Crispy steamed mange-touts

Hot mint soufflé with chocolate sauce

Of course, you really should have started preparing for this meal by making the lemon gin at the beginning of summer! I 'discovered' lemon gin by accident. We are not gin drinkers, but we bought a bottle on the plane home from Sicily.

So, since I have always considered gin quite a good spirit for cooking both fish and fowl, I decided to flavour it. I peeled the zest in long strips from two or three lemons and put them into the half-bottle of gin. Some weeks later, I had a fragrant pale yellow gin, tasting of essence of lemons.

Starting from scratch, it works quite well if you grate the lemon zest into some heated gin and let it steep for a few hours or overnight.

It has taken me a long time to come round to the idea of serving chicken as a special occasion dish. I find the flesh of supermarket frozen chickens soggy, dense and lacking any 'chicken' flavour. Look for free-range farm chickens. If they have been fed on good things the chances

are they will taste good. I buy maize-fed chickens from France, now available in large chainstores. Some are supplied by local farms; we should encourage them.

It might sound extravagant to buy whole chickens when all you want to use is the breast, but it isn't really when you consider that you will have fine carcasses and trimmings to make stock; wings and drumsticks to marinate in spicy sauce then grill or barbecue; and thighs to casserole or curry.

The chicken breast makes a pretty dish, presented on an individual plate with a little vegetable purée and, for contrast, a crisp green vegetable.

The preceding dish, fresh pasta parcels of scallops, will present few problems, even to those who have never made their own pasta before. All you need is a long rolling pin, patience and room to roll out the dough.

This is a meal full of delicate flavours and textures. I think

German wines would complement the dishes perfectly. I would serve a Moselle with the scallops, and then move on to a Rheingau, a rather more full-bodied wine, with the chicken. The 1983 vintage is particularly good and this is the one I would go for; but if it were a really special occasion I think I would serve one of the great 1976 Rheingaus: a Hallgarten Mehrhölzchen Riesling from Schloss Rheinhartshausen.

With the strongly flavoured pudding sparkling mineral water or a good cognac would be my choice, because few wines can stand up to mint and chocolate. However, I have tried a well-chilled Charbaut rosé champagne with the soufflé, and it worked well.

COUNTDOWN

The day before
• *Infuse gin with lemon.*
• *Make sugar syrup for soufflé and infuse with mint.*

In the afternoon
• *Make pasta and stuff.*

Two hours before
• *Remove breasts from chickens and chill.*

An hour and a half before
• *Make carrot purée.*
• *Blanch mint leaves, and strain syrup.*
• *Prepare moulds.*
• *Blend syrup and mint leaves. Blend again with egg yolks.*

Half an hour before
• *Boil water for pasta.*
• *Fry scallops.*
• *Cook pasta.*
• *Cook chicken breasts and keep hot.*
• *Reheat carrot purée.*

After the first course
• *Heat oven to 200C/400F/ gas 6.*
• *Deglaze pan in which chicken was cooked with gin and stock and complete sauce.*
• *Plate chicken and sauce.*
• *Steam the mange-touts.*

After the main course
• *Whisk egg whites and fold into syrup mixture. Bake soufflés.*
• *Melt chocolate.*

Breasts of chicken with dill and lemon gin sauce, carrot purée and crispy steamed mange-touts

PARCELS OF PASTA WITH SCALLOPS AND SAFFRON SAUCE

SERVES 6

200g/7oz strong white flour
2 size 3 eggs
few drops of oil
FOR THE FILLING AND SAUCE
10 large scallops with big corals
400ml/14fl. oz home-made fish stock
pinch of saffron threads
3 tablespoons finely chopped shallots
salt and pepper
25g/1oz unsalted butter (optional)
fresh coriander, basil, chervil or parsley to garnish

1. You can make the dough very easily if you have a food processor. Put the flour into the bowl, add the eggs and process in short bursts for 30 seconds. The texture will be crumbly and soft. Scoop it all together and mould it into a ball. Let it rest covered in cling film in a cool place for 10-15 minutes.

2. If you make the dough by hand, heap the flour on to a marble slab or cool surface. Make a well in the centre of the flour and slide in the eggs. Work into a dough with your fingertips and form it into a ball. Let it rest covered in cling film in a cool place for 10-15 minutes.

3. Cut off a piece the size of an egg and roll it out as thinly as possible on a lightly floured surface; it should be no thicker than a 20p piece. I find it easier to roll out 1 small piece of dough at a time. Keep the remaining pasta covered to prevent it from drying out.

4. When you have a sheet of thin pasta, stamp out circles with a pastry cutter, 5-10cm/2-4in diameter. The size is not particularly important — if you cut out large ones, you'll probably only want 2 per serving, 4 or 5 if small. Place the pasta rounds in a single layer and not touching, on a board or tray covered with a clean tea towel; cover them with another barely damp tea towel while you prepare the filling and the sauce.

5. Prepare the scallops by separating the coral (also called the tongue or the roe) from the white part. Remove the thin dark intestine which encircles the scallop and the small cushion of muscle (which toughens during cooking if not removed). Wash quickly to remove any sand, and dry thoroughly. Slice 6 of the scallops into 2 or 3 rounds and chop the remaining 4 into tiny pieces.

6. Heat the fish stock in a pan, then pour 3 tablespoons into a small bowl or teacup and steep the saffron threads. Boil the chopped shallot in the remaining stock until soft. Strain the stock and reserve the shallots.

7. To make the stuffing, chop the corals on a board until you have a thick paste. Mix in the shallots and the chopped white scallop meat. Lightly season with freshly ground white pepper and the merest hint of salt.

8. Uncover the pasta circles. Taking them one by one, spoon about 1 teaspoon of stuffing on to each circle. Dampen the edges, fold over and seal firmly into a half-moon shape. Place them back on the tray and cover until required. You can prepare up to this point several hours in advance. I usually do these in the afternoon before a dinner party. It is not something that can be left until the last minute.

9. To finish the dish, bring a large pan of lightly salted water to the boil, and add a drop or two of oil to prevent the pasta from sticking together.

10. Meanwhile, melt the butter in a frying pan or heat a non-stick frying pan; quickly fry the sliced scallops for 30 seconds on both sides, remove and keep in a warm place. Add the stock and the strained saffron liquid to the pan. Allow to boil quite fiercely and reduce it to about 300ml/½pt of sauce.

11. Drop the pasta parcels into the boiling water. Bring back to the boil and cook for 2-3 minutes until just tender. Drain.

12. Pour some sauce on to each heated serving plate and place the pasta parcels on top. Arrange 2 or 3 slices of scallop around them and garnish with fresh herbs. Drizzle a little more sauce over the pasta.

Parcels of pasta with scallops and saffron sauce

BREASTS OF CHICKEN WITH DILL AND LEMON GIN SAUCE

SERVES 6

50ml/2fl. oz gin
2 lemons with unblemished skins
6 chicken breasts, removed from 3 whole chickens
50g/2oz unsalted butter (optional)
150ml/¼pt home-made chicken stock
1 bunch of dill, chopped
50ml/2fl. oz double cream or crème fraîche (optional)
sprigs of dill to garnish

1. Heat the gin to just below boiling point. Grate the lemon zest into it and allow to infuse for a few hours or overnight.

2. Remove the skin from the chicken breasts and trim off any sinews, fat and gristle. Melt the butter in the frying pan or, preferably, heat a non-stick frying pan. Place the chicken breasts in a single layer in the pan and cook on one side for 5-8 minutes.

3. Remove the chicken breasts when done, and keep hot. Add the lemon gin and the stock to the frying pan; stir to deglaze. Add the dill and reduce the sauce until quite syrupy in texture. Stir in the cream if you want a creamy opaque sauce, rather than a translucent one.

4. To serve, slice the chicken breasts diagonally and serve them fanned out on each plate, garnished with the fronds of dill, sitting in a pool of sauce.

CARROT PURÉE

SERVES 6

250g/8oz carrots
250g/8oz potatoes
3 heads garlic
6 cardamom pods

1. Cut the potatoes and carrots into chunks and boil them together with the garlic and the seeds from the cardamom pods. When the vegetables are soft, drain, then mash or process.

HOT MINT SOUFFLÉ WITH CHOCOLATE SAUCE

SERVES 6

150g/5oz sugar
1 bunch fresh mint
4 eggs
butter for greasing
caster sugar for dusting
150g/5oz plain chocolate

1. Make a syrup by melting the sugar in 300ml/½pt water; bring it to the boil and cook rapidly for 12 minutes until reduced by half. Strip the mint leaves from the stalks and add half of them to the syrup. Stir in and leave overnight.

2. Next day, blanch the rest of the mint leaves: place them in a sieve and pour boiling water over them. Strain the syrup, then blend it in a liquidizer with the freshly blanched mint leaves to make a light, frothy, green syrup.

3. Separate the eggs and add 2 yolks to the syrup (keep the other 2 for another recipe), blend again. Grease 6 small ramekins with butter and dust with caster sugar.

4. Heat the oven to 200C/400F/gas 6. Whisk all the egg whites until stiff and fold into the liquid. Pour into the ramekins. Stand the ramekins in a baking tray and pour in boiling water to reach three-quarters up the sides. Bake for 18 minutes in the oven.

5. Meanwhile, melt the chocolate in a *bain-marie*, or in a basin over a pan of hot water. Pour the melted chocolate into a jug.

6. Serve the soufflés immediately. Each person makes a hole in the top with a teaspoon and pours in a little melted chocolate.

WINE NOTES

Few cooks are as specific in their wine choice as Frances Bissell has been, and I am quite sure her ideas will work triumphantly well. Taste has sometimes expressed disappointment at the general standard of German wines available in Britain, but bear in mind that there is a world of difference between estate-bottled German wine from the fine vineyards of the leading estates and indifferent overcropped and over-sweetened wines that have made up the bulk of exports hitherto.

The Rheingau estates, in whose vintage wines I have implicit faith, include besides Mrs Bissell's nomination – Schloss Rheinhartshausen – the Winzergenossenschaft Erbach, Erben J. Fischer, Langwerth von Simmern and H. H. Eser. For the Moselle, leading producers with names to trust are the Friedrich Wilhelm Gymnasium, Reichsgraf von Kesselstatt, C. von Schubert and above all, J. J. Prum.

For pink champagne, Taste preference is still for Fliniaux NV or, failing that, Laurent-Perrier or Pol Roger. For the more economically minded, pink Crémant de Bourgogne is a very acceptable substitute.

AUTUMN

*C*risp autumn days bring ripening berries — brambles, sloes and elder — glinting in the hedgerows, apple boughs hanging heavy with their fat rosy fruits, and nuts falling softly to the ground. The harvest is safely gathered in and the stubble gleams in the sunshine, greedily gobbled by geese, where permitted, in what was once an everyday, every-village, sight. Revive the old tradition of a Michaelmas goose with Hilary Walden's dinner, warmly finished with fresh English cheeses and a medieval frumenty.

The earthy tastes of autumn are highlighted by Giuliano Bugialli in his dish of bulb fennel masked with a sweet tomato sauce, and a rich, rich coffee-nut cake gilded with a coffee zabaione. Game, of course, is autumn's great treat, and Harvey Sambrook suggests a wonderfully indulgent lunch with pheasant in port sauce accompanied by chicory, another earthy-tasting vegetable (too rarely cooked), fluffed into a 'mousse'. Autumn's fruits he spices with cinnamon and red wine to give a warming fruit salad. Glynn Christian reflects the season's rich colours — and ingredients — in his luscious menu based on gold and jewels: turkey breasts in a coat of fresh cranberries and pecan nuts; the magical pumpkin souffléed with sweet allspice, and a gleaming coconut and chocolate truffle loaf laced with nuggets of pineapple.

After all this richness, Sonia Blech prepares for the Christmas onslaught with a wonderfully light but very elegant dinner. A colourful mosaic of carrot and avocado, delicate parcels of halibut and salmon, and a refreshing citrus fruit and sabayon brulée provide the perfect balance of autumn warmth and a touch of sharpness, in a fine farewell to the season.

Hilary Walden

MICHAELMAS DINNER

St Michael's Day, 29 September, heralds the arrival of autumn, and Hilary Walden celebrates with the ancient custom of serving a goose

---

Poached perch

Michaelmas goose with sage and onion stuffing and apple sauce
Spinach with lightly sautéed sorrel; steamed new potatoes in their jackets; braised red cabbage

---

Green salad; seasonal cheeses including Blue Vinny, Stilton and Caerphilly

---

Frumenty

Eating goose on Michaelmas Day is supposed to ensure good luck and prosperity for the coming year — a prospect that certainly appeals to me and is sufficient reason to hold a Michaelmas dinner.

Michaelmas, or St Michael's Day (29 September), was one of the many church fast days which forbade the consumption of meat. Goose, however, could be eaten as it was classed originally as wildfowl. Also, Michaelmas Day is one of the four quarter days on which three-monthly, and often annual, rents fall due.

It became the custom for farming tenants to give their landlords a present in lieu of, or as well as, their rent. And what better present than a goose? It would be particularly good eating at Michaelmas time. After the harvest, geese were moved from their summer grazing to the corn fields to supplement their diet with wheat stubble and gleanings. They gained extra flavour but not too much fat.

Queen Elizabeth I is said to have been eating her customary roast Michaelmas goose when she learnt of the defeat of the Spanish Armada, and decreed that goose should always be served on the anniversary to commemorate the victory.

The traditional accompaniments to a Michaelmas goose — apple sauce, sage and onion stuffing and frumenty — were natural choices as they were made from foods that were in season at the same time. The apple season was at its height, and bruised windfalls could be put to good use in a sauce for the goose. Onions were being lifted and those that had gone to seed were combined with the last of the sage to make a stuffing. The soft grains of freshly gathered or gleaned wheat could be used to make frumenty, without the need for grinding them into flour.

Rabbits were easily spotted in the newly bare fields. They were tasty and plump from eating stolen corn, and less speedy so they could be caught easily. Less-well-off country folk would cook rabbit along with the goose to make it go further.

A couple of rabbit legs packed into the bird's cavity, or placed under it while it is cooking, absorb the flavour and some of the character of the goose. The leaner flesh of the rabbit provides a contrast to that of the goose — and, I think, is a very good substitute for many conventional stuffings, especially those based on sausage meat.

I have chosen perch to precede the goose. Its light but fine-textured flesh and delicate flavour are shown off to best advantage by simple cooking. Perch used to be the most popular fish stocked in the ponds and lakes of monasteries and country houses. They could also be caught for free by country folk in streams and rivers. They are not seen for sale very often, so it is necessary to order them (they do appear at Billingsgate, so a good fishmonger should have no problem if given warning).

By Michaelmas a goose would be about six months old and have reached a weight of about 3.6kg/8lb. When the accompaniments, including the rabbit, are taken into account, it should serve about eight people.

For this meal I would choose good, but not great, wines. I don't need much of an excuse for having a reasonable champagne as an aperitif; with the fish I would serve a good white burgundy, but not a

powerful one because of the delicacy of perch — or perhaps an Alsace Riesling. With the goose, a Rheinpfalz Spätlese or an Alsace *réserve exceptionelle* would be interesting. But I would probably opt for a claret.

POACHED PERCH

Perch are covered with many coarse scales which are difficult to remove when the fish is raw, but can easily be lifted off with the skin after cooking. This takes time just before the meal is served, but I think is worth it; cooking the fish whole with the skin keeps the flesh moist and preserves the flavour. It also lessens the danger of breaking up if you let them overcook. If you can't find perch, use carp or rainbow trout.

SERVES 8

4 perch, 600g/1¼lb each or 2 weighing 1.1kg/2½lb each
2 shallots, finely chopped
1 leek, white part only, finely chopped
1 small carrot, chopped
bunch of herbs including a sprig of thyme, 4 parsley sprigs and a small sprig of rosemary
about 850ml/1½pt well-flavoured fish stock
300ml/½pt medium-bodied dry white wine
salt and freshly ground pepper
25g/1oz cold, unsalted butter, cut into small pieces
salad leaves and herbs to garnish

1. Carefully gut the perch. Wipe the cavities with absorbent paper but do not rinse them. Make a bed of the chopped shallots, leek, carrot and herbs in the bottom of a large saucepan, frying pan or flameproof casserole. (If you don't have a pan large enough to hold all the fish, use two and divide the ingredients between them.) Put the fish in a single layer on top.
2. Mix the stock and wine together and pour over the fish, adding more stock if necessary almost to cover them. Season

COUNTDOWN

Two weeks before
• *Order the goose and perch.*

The night before
• *Start cooking the wheat for the frumenty.*

In the morning
• *Prepare the fish and giblet stocks.*
• *Prepare the red cabbage and the stuffing, and stuff the goose.*

About four hours before
• *Start cooking the goose.*
• *Prepare the salad leaves and the dressing.*

About two-and-a-half hours before
• *Put the cabbage to braise on the shelf below the goose.*

One hour before the guests arrive
• *Get the pan or pans ready with vegetables, stock and wine for the fish.*
• *Boil down the red wine and stock for the sauce to serve with the goose. Put the rabbit legs into the goose.*
• *Start to cook the apple sauce.*
• *Finish cooking the frumenty and keep it warm.*

About 15-20 minutes before the meal
• *Start cooking the fish.*
• *Add the diced apple to the apple sauce.*
• *Remove the goose from the roasting tin and leave it in the oven with the heat turned off.*
• *Put the potatoes to steam.*

After the first course
• *Cook the spinach and sorrel.*
• *Make the sauce for the goose. Take the goose to the table to carve.*

After the main course
• *Toss the salad.*

and bring to the boil. Skim off any surface scum as it rises. Reduce the heat so the liquid barely simmers, cover the pan and cook the fish for about 12-15 minutes for 600g/1¼lb size fish, 18-20 minutes for 1.1kg/2½lb, or until the flesh by the backbone only just flakes easily. Carefully lift the fish from the pan; cover and keep warm. Boil the cooking juices until they are well reduced and become slightly syrupy.

3. Meanwhile, cut the head and tail from one perch and carefully remove the skin from the upper side. Run the point of a sharp knife along the backbone. Carefully lift off the top fillet. Lift away the backbone and bones attached to it. Lift the fillet underneath away from the skin. Place the fillets on a warmed serving plate. Cover and keep warm while you fillet the remaining fish in the same way.

4. Pour the reduced cooking juices through a fine sieve. Reheat; taste and adjust the seasoning. If necessary, boil to reduce further; alternatively dilute with extra fish stock or wine. Whisk in the butter, piece by piece, until each is absorbed into the sauce. Spoon some of the sauce over each fillet and serve garnished with salad leaves and herbs.

MICHAELMAS GOOSE

In 1817, cookery writer Dr Kitchener proclaimed that 'Goose at Michaelmas is as famous in the mouths of the millions, as the minced pie at Christmas . . .'. Nowadays, only about five per cent of all the geese reared are eaten for this festival, so you will have to order a fresh one from a poulterer a week or two in advance. To avoid spending too much time in the kitchen at the last moment, you can partially reduce the wine and stock for the sauce beforehand.

SERVES 8

3.6-4kg/8-9lb goose, with giblets
salt and freshly ground pepper
2 rabbit hind-leg portions
3 tablespoons brandy, optional
600ml/1pt red wine
850ml/1½pt stock made with the giblets
25g/1oz cold, unsalted butter, diced

1. Heat the oven to 200C/400F/gas 6. Remove any stray feathers or quills from the goose (and the wing tips and feet at first joint). Remove the visible fat inside the cavity and around the vent — there will not be as much as in a

goose killed at Christmas time. Wipe the outside and rinse the inside thoroughly several times. Dry well. Prick the fatty parts of lower legs, breast, between the breast and legs and the sides of the bird so as not to pierce the flesh. Season the bird inside and out and fill the neck end with sage and onion stuffing (see following recipe). Truss the goose neatly and place it, breast uppermost, on a fairly high rack in a roasting tin. Roast the goose for 20 minutes.

2. Turn the bird over on to its breast and cook for a further 30 minutes. Drain off and reserve the fat that has collected in the cavity and prick the skin once more. Reduce the oven temperature to 170C/325F/gas 3 and cook for a further 3 hours or until the juices that flow from the fleshy part of the leg run clear when tested with a fine skewer. Turn the bird so that it cooks for the first 35 minutes on one side, the next 35 minutes on the other, and the remainder of the time breast uppermost.

3. About 1 hour before the end of cooking, insert the seasoned rabbit inside the cavity. Close it with a skewer. 20 minutes before the end of the cooking, increase the temperature to about 220C/425F/gas 7. Pour off the fat in the cavity and sprinkle the skin with cold water to brown and crisp it.

4. Remove the goose, still on the rack, from the roasting tin. Cover with a dome of foil and keep it warm in the oven with the heat turned off.

5. Make the sauce. Pour off the excess fat from the roasting tin; place the tin over a moderate heat and stir in the brandy, if using, to dislodge the sediment. Ignite the brandy and when the flames have died down, stir in the wine and boil again until reduced to about 75ml/3fl. oz. Stir in the stock and boil until reduced to about 450ml/¾pt. Reduce the heat and gradually stir in the butter, fully incorporating each piece before adding the next. Adjust the seasoning and strain into a warmed sauceboat. Serve the goose with apple sauce (see recipe), steamed new potatoes in their jackets, spinach and sorrel, and braised red cabbage.

SAGE AND ONION STUFFING

Traditionally, stuffings were cooked with the goose to make it go further and to soak up the rich juices — I serve French bread, as well, for this purpose. Sage was served with goose to help the digestion and to counteract the richness of the flesh.

25g/1oz unsalted butter, diced
2 large onions, chopped
100g/4oz fresh white breadcrumbs
squeeze of lemon juice
2 tablespoons chopped fresh sage
beaten egg, to bind the mixture
salt and freshly ground pepper

1. Melt the butter; add the onions and cook, covered, over a low heat until softened but not coloured. Stir in the breadcrumbs, lemon juice, sage, egg and seasonings and leave to cool completely. Use to fill the neck end of the goose.

APPLE SAUCE

The sharpness of the apples contrasts with the richness of the goose. With nutmeg and cinnamon, this recipe has a slight hint of sweet spices.

SERVES 8

1kg/2lb Bramley's seedling cooking apples
5 tablespoons lemon juice
large pinch of freshly grated nutmeg
large pinch of cinnamon
freshly ground pepper
40g/1½oz unsalted butter, diced
muscovado sugar to taste (optional)

1. Peel, core and dice the apples. Mix about a quarter of the dice with 2 tablespoons lemon juice and reserve. Put the remaining chopped apple into an ovenproof dish; toss with the rest of the lemon juice and the spices, then dot the butter over the top. Cover the dish and cook the apples alongside the goose for 45-60 minutes or until the apples are just soft.

2. Break up the apple with a spoon — it should be knobbly rather than smooth — and add a little sugar to taste, if necessary. Scatter with the reserved apple, cover again and return the dish to the oven for about 10 more minutes. Stir well, then spoon the sauce into a warmed dish.

Note:

You could use dessert apples, which do not need sugar.

FRUMENTY

Frumenty dates from early medieval times, when it was served as an accompaniment to game and meat by the rich, but provided a complete meal for the poor. Later on, it became a dessert, sweetened by honey and dried fruits, to add flavour and texture to the porridge-like dish.

Cream and whisky make the frumenty more luxurious and suitable for a dinner party. Serve in small bowls as it is rich and filling. In Scotland it is made with oatmeal rather than wheat.

SERVES 8

200g/7oz whole wheat grains
400ml/14fl. oz milk, plus extra for thinning if necessary
75ml/3fl. oz double cream
175g/6oz mixed dried fruit such as pears, peaches, apricots and figs, chopped
long strip of lemon zest
3 tablespoons whisky
honey to taste (optional)
lemon juice (optional)
cream to serve

1. Put the wheat into a large casserole and pour in warm water to cover generously. Cover the dish tightly and place in a very low oven, 110C/225F/gas ¼, for about 12 hours.

2. Drain the wheat in a colander, then tip into a saucepan. Stir in the milk, cream, dried fruit and lemon zest, and bring slowly to the boil, still stirring. Reduce the heat to very low and cook gently for about 20-25 minutes, stirring frequently, until nearly all the liquid has been absorbed.

3. Remove the lemon zest and stir in the whisky. Transfer it to a heatproof pudding basin. Cover basin and place in a saucepan of hot water to keep warm until required. Thin the frumenty with a little extra hot milk, if necessary, and serve the honey, lemon juice and cream separately.

Frumenty with honey and cream

WINE NOTES

Reasonable aperitif champagne is not hard to find: the standards of supermarket and merchants' own label wines are generally quite high, and competition is keen, though – as noted before – the wines' characteristics are not necessarily consistent over long periods of time. Laurent-Perrier is often the best value for money of the top-quality grandes marques.

With Alsace wines – still likely to be far better bargains than white burgundies – do not scorn the production of the co-operatives. Bennwihr, Eguisheim, and Beblenheim are dependable, and Turckheim brilliant. The house of Hugel, though, pioneered the richer Réserve Personnelle *wines, and make them sensationally good.*

With goose I would prefer the full-bodied, spicy flavours and oily texture of Tokay d'Alsace or Gewürztraminer to the steely acidity of Riesling. Everyone thinks of goose as fatty meat, but the fat is superficial and tends to run off in the cooking: the lean meat is surprisingly dry and needs plenty of fruity flavour.

For red wines, there is a clutch of recent good Bordeaux vintages to choose from, at undemanding prices. Choose a petit château *wine in these days of surprisingly numerous good vintages and you are unlikely to be disappointed. Lead on to something more substantial (from the great 1982 vintage possibly) and you can finish the meal on a high note with the cheese.*

Giuliano Bugialli

ITALIAN DINNER PARTY

As the autumn evenings close in, succumb to the earthy magic of Italian food with Giuliano Bugialli's mouthwatering dinner party menu

---

Spaghetti al limone
Spaghetti with lemon cream

Salsiccia di pollo al pepe verde
Galantine of chicken with green peppercorn sauce

Finocchi in sugo
Fennel in tomato sauce

Dolce di caffe
Coffee-nut cake
Zabaione di caffe
Coffee zabaione

Despite the recent innovation and creativity in food preparation and service, smart Italian dining has retained its strict classical order of courses. Aperitifs are served as the guests stand around talking. In recent years dry white wine has increasingly replaced the herb-flavoured pre-dinner drinks once so popular — accompanied, if at all, by salted nuts.

If there is a hot or cold antipasto, it is eaten at the table and accompanied by a new wine, a white or a light red. Since this wine is usually carried over to the *primo piatto*, the next course, it is selected to blend well with both dishes. The *primo piatto*, which literally means the first course, may be pasta, soup or a rice preparation such as risotto. In older and stricter times, this was not accompanied by wine, but the present-day compromise has been simply to continue with the wine of the antipasto course.

The dinner presented here, with four courses, contains a separate vegetable dish, so we are omitting the antipasto. In general, Italians prefer not to have too many courses and also to limit the number of wines (not the amount!), so the meal is a balanced ensemble.

We begin with a pasta (freshly made or dried spaghetti), dressed with a light lemon cream sauce of

Spaghetti al limone, *spaghetti with lemon cream*

COUNTDOWN

During the day

• *Make the coffee-nut cake and when cold, store it in a tin.*
• *Make the tomato sauce, cook the fennel, and combine the two in an ovenproof dish. Cover and chill.*
• *Skin the chicken and make the stock. Make the galantine, roll it up, wrap it in foil and put it in the refrigerator.*
• *Make the green peppercorn sauce for the galantine, cover the top with greaseproof paper to prevent a skin forming, and refrigerate.*
• *Make the zabaione and refrigerate.*

An hour and a half before the meal

• *Heat the oven to 190C/375F/ gas 5 and bake the galantine.*
• *Grate the lemon zest and Parmesan ready for the pasta.*
• *Chill the white wine, and open the red.*

Twenty minutes before the meal

• *Remove the galantine from the oven and leave it, wrapped, in a warm place.*
• *Turn the oven down to 170C/ 325F/gas 3 and heat the fennel in tomato sauce.*
• *Warm the serving dishes and plates.*

Fifteen minutes before the meal

• *Cook the pasta and its sauce.*

After the first course

• *Heat the green peppercorn sauce.*
• *Unwrap the galantine, slice it and serve.*

delicate flavour. I have selected a crisp but full-bodied white wine from south-west Piedmont, Gavi di Gavi, to accompany it. Its bouquet blends well with both the cream and the lemon.

The *secondo piatto*, or main course, chicken galantine with green peppercorn sauce, carries forward the acidity of the lemon but reinforces it with the spiciness of green peppercorns in brine. Rather than an abrupt contrast in taste, we have a transition and intensification. The red wine accompanying it is the young Brusco of the Brunello area, Montalcino in Tuscany. It is bright enough not to overpower the galantine, but full enough not to be itself overcome by the peppery sauce, and is a complex, lively and remarkably harmonious wine for one so young. It does credit to its older brother Brunello.

The vegetable course is not served with the main course. It is too important for this, and occupies the position of what Italians traditionally call the *piatto di mezzo*, an independent in-between course. Vegetables are treated with respect in Italian cooking, so that even when one accompanies a main dish, it stands on its own and is served on a separate plate.

Our fennel in tomato sauce gives variety to the palate, the sweetness of the tomatoes helping to neutralize any pepper that remains from the previous dish. This sweet flavour will bring out a completely different aspect of the Brusco. A fuller wine like Barolo would not have this adaptability.

There is no salad course, because salad is served in place of the vegetable only when it matches the main course, for instance with grilled steak or a deep-fried dish.

The meal in Italy finishes with fruit, cheese or a combination of the two, or with dessert. The rich almond and walnut cake is paired here with a coffee-flavoured

zabaione, whose creamy texture returns us to the opening dish of the dinner. Despite the coffee flavour, the cake would be accompanied by a dessert wine such as *vin santo*.

Coffee is served after the meal, usually in another room. An after-dinner *digestivo* such as Amaro Averna is more traditional than brandy or sweet cordials, and may be served with the coffee (espresso, of course, never cappuccino).

SPAGHETTI AL LIMONE
Spaghetti with lemon cream

Even if you have tried pasta with cream and lemon before, this sauce will come as a magnificent surprise.

SERVES 6

700g/1½lb fresh pasta, or 500g/1lb dried spaghetti
salt
FOR THE SAUCE
175g/6oz unsalted butter
450ml/¾pt double cream
grated zest of 2 thick-skinned lemons
salt and white pepper
pinch of freshly grated nutmeg
175-200g/6-7oz freshly grated Parmesan
15 small sprigs of flat-leaved parsley

1. Bring a large pan of water to the boil. While the water heats, balance a large frying pan with the butter in it over the pan so that the butter melts. When the water starts to boil and the butter has melted, add salt to the water, then the pasta, and cook it for 1-3 minutes if fresh, 9-12 minutes if dried, until just firm to the bite — *al dente*.
2. Drain the pasta and add it to the melted butter in the frying pan. Put the pan over medium heat, add the cream, lemon zest, salt, pepper and nutmeg. Mix very well and let the sauce reduce for 2 minutes, then add the Parmesan.
3. Mix again and transfer to a warmed serving platter. Sprinkle with the parsley and serve immediately.

SALSICCIA DI POLLO AL PEPE VERDE
Galantine of chicken with green peppercorn sauce

A sausage made from minced chicken spiked with peppercorns, served warm with a creamy peppercorn sauce.

SERVES 6

1 whole chicken, weighing about 1.5kg/3¼lb
100g/4oz prosciutto, sliced very thinly
350g/12oz lean minced pork
225ml/8fl. oz double cream
salt
1 scant tablespoon green peppercorns in brine, drained, rinsed and lightly crushed
olive oil for greasing
FOR THE GREEN PEPPERCORN SAUCE
1 level tablespoon green peppercorns in brine, drained and rinsed
4 tablespoons olive oil
salt
25g/1oz unsalted butter, at room temperature
1 tablespoon plain flour
450ml/¾pt home-made chicken stock, lukewarm
1 garlic clove, peeled and finely chopped

1. First skin the chicken. Remove the last 2 joints from each wing, the ends of the leg joints and the parson's nose — use them to make the stock. Cut through the 2 tendons at the end of each of the legs. Cut the skin lengthways down the backbone. Use a paring knife and, pushing your hand in beneath the skin, lift it in one piece. A clean tea towel helps to give a better grip. Take particular care around the breast bone, where the skin can tear.

2. Spread out the skin on a board, inside upward. Cover it completely with the prosciutto slices. Remove the breast meat from the chicken and mince it coarsely. (Reserve the remainder of the bird for another dish.) Add the minced pork and then the cream, and season with salt. Mix all the ingredients together well with a wooden spoon. Add the crushed peppercorns and mix again.

3. Put the stuffing on one end of the prepared skin and roll it up like a sausage, overlapping the skin. Oil the shiny side of a large piece of aluminium foil and place the chicken galantine on it. Wrap it like a parcel, seal firmly and chill for 30 minutes.

4. Heat the oven to 190C/375F/gas 5. Bake the galantine parcel for 1 hour, turning it once. Remove from the oven and leave it in a warm place to rest, wrapped, for 30 minutes.

5. Meanwhile, prepare the sauce. Finely chop the peppercorns and transfer to a small, heavy pan. Add the oil and salt to taste; mix well and simmer gently for 5 minutes, stirring occasionally.

6. Melt the butter in a small pan and stir in the flour; cook gently for 1 minute then slowly stir in some of the chicken stock, off the heat. Return to the heat and stir in the remaining stock. Bring to the boil, stirring. Add the peppercorns in the oil to the sauce, with the garlic, and mix well. Simmer for 10 minutes, until the sauce has reduced and thickened.

7. When the sauce is ready, unwrap the meat and cut it into 12 slices. To serve, place 2 slices on a plate and spoon sauce beside them.

FINOCCHI IN SUGO
Fennel in tomato sauce

The distinctive taste of fennel is made slightly sweeter by being baked in a tomato sauce.

SERVES 6

6 fennel bulbs, weighing about 175/6oz each
1 tablespoon flour
6 tablespoons olive oil
salt and freshly ground pepper
FOR THE TOMATO SAUCE
1kg/2lb fresh tomatoes, or 800g/ 1lb 14oz canned tomatoes, with their juice
2 garlic cloves
4 tablespoons olive oil
10 basil leaves
salt and freshly ground pepper

1. First, prepare the tomato sauce. Chop the tomatoes roughly and put them in a small saucepan over medium heat, with the garlic, oil and basil. Cook for 20 minutes, stirring every so often with a wooden spoon. Press the contents of the pan through a food mill, using the disc with the smallest holes, into a bowl.
2. Remove the outside layer from the fennel, then cut each bulb lengthways into 4 slices. Place the slices in a bowl of cold water for about 15 minutes, then remove and dry on absorbent paper.
3. Sprinkle the flour over the fennel pieces through a sieve. Heat half the olive oil in a large frying pan, add half the fennel slices and sauté them, turning once, until golden brown all over (about 3-4 minutes each side). Sprinkle with salt and pepper. Cook the remaining fennel in the same way.
4. Return all the fennel to the pan, add the tomato sauce, season well and simmer gently for 15 minutes, loosening the fennel pieces with a spatula now and then so they do not stick. Alternatively, put the fennel in an ovenproof dish with the tomato sauce, cover it tightly with foil and put it in a low oven (170C/ 325F/gas 3) for up to 30 minutes. Serve very hot.

DOLCE DI CAFFE
Coffee-nut cake

This cake is plain, but has a good flavour. It can be served warm or cold, with chilled coffee-flavoured zabaione, a rich egg sauce (see recipe below).

SERVES 6

100ml/3½fl. oz strong coffee, preferably Italian espresso
4 tablespoons unsweetened cocoa powder
4 eggs, separated
7 tablespoons granulated sugar
75g/3oz blanched almonds
75g/3oz walnuts

1. Heat the coffee over medium heat until lukewarm. Pour it over the cocoa powder in a small bowl, and stir very well with a wooden spoon until the cocoa is completely dissolved. Leave it until cold (about 30 minutes).
2. Place the egg yolks in a large bowl, add 4 tablespoons of the sugar and whisk until the sugar is completely absorbed and the yolks thicken and turn a lighter colour. Add the cold coffee-cocoa mixture and stir well.
3. Heat the oven to 190C/375F/gas 5. Finely grind together the almonds, walnuts and the remaining 3 tablespoons sugar, then add them to the egg mixture. Butter a 20cm/8in cake tin, line the base with buttered greaseproof paper, and flour the inside of the tin.
4. Preferably using a copper bowl and wire whisk, whisk the egg whites until stiff. Gently fold them into the egg and nut mixture with a metal spoon, using a figure-of-eight motion. Pour into the prepared tin and bake for 45 minutes or until firm to the touch.
5. Remove the cake tin from the oven and leave it for 5 minutes before unmoulding the cake on to a rack to cool for 20 minutes (longer if you wish to serve it cold). Place the cake on a serving dish, slice it and serve, spooning some of the coffee-flavoured zabaione (see following recipe) on one side of the dish.

WINE NOTES

Gavi di Gavi La Scolca is often claimed to be Italy's finest dry white wine, but it is punishingly priced. There are cheaper alternatives, but all Gavi, and wines from the Cortese grape, seem to me over-expensive. I would go instead for a pale and fresh Bianco di Custoza or any decent Italian Pinot Grigio.

Brusco dei Barbi is imported to Britain, but if it is not easily found acceptable alternatives would be Rosso di Montalcino or a young Valpolicella Classico.

Italy's finest vin santo, a really delicious wine, is made by Avignonesi but it justifiably commands a high price. Any Italian delicatessen might stock a more modest example, possibly an interesting one from an individual grower.

Amaro Averna, a bittersweet herb and almond digestive, has a pleasanter and easier finish than the more familiar Fernet-Branca.

ZABAIONE DI CAFFE
Coffee zabaione

SERVES 6

3 egg yolks
3 tablespoons granulated sugar
100ml/3½fl. oz strong coffee, preferably Italian espresso, cold
350ml/12fl. oz double cream
3 tablespoons caster sugar
1 tablespoon icing sugar

1. Prepare a double boiler with barely simmering (not boiling) water. Place the egg yolks in a bowl with the granulated sugar. Whisk until the sugar is completely incorporated and the yolks turn a lighter colour. Add the cold coffee slowly, mixing steadily, then stand the bowl on the double boiler, making sure that it does not touch the water.

2. Whisk constantly until the zabaione is thick, doubled in bulk and will coat the whisk beaters.

3. Immediately remove the bowl from the heat and whisk the contents for another 2 or 3 minutes, then transfer the zabaione to another bowl to cool (this will take about an hour).

4. When it is cold, using a chilled metal bowl and a wire whisk, whip the cream with the caster sugar and icing sugar, and fold the zabaione into it. Cover the bowl and refrigerate until needed – but not overnight or it could drop.

Harvey Sambrook

LATE AUTUMN LUNCH

Serve Harvey Sambrook's warming menu to combat chilly autumn days

---

Grilled pink grapefruit with honey

Scallops Chinoise

Pheasant in port sauce with chicory 'mousse'

Roquefort, Stilton and Camembert with green salad

Autumn fruit salad in wine

I have always loved the autumn. There may still be sunny days to enjoy, but you can also justify lighting the fire in the evening. Oysters are back, game is in, and you don't look too eccentric if you offer your friends a steamed pudding.

Having spent too much time in my own restaurants over the years, I now prefer to entertain at home. I also like to talk to my friends while I'm cooking. Fortunately, we have a large kitchen-cum-living-room where we entertain a couple of times a week. This layout allows me to chat and cook at the same time – I'm far too disorganized to have everything prepared in advance. Entertaining this way also allows a natural break between courses which, I believe, helps both relaxation and digestion.

This lunch may look fairly elaborate but, like almost all cooking, it really is simple if you take a little care about timing and heat control.

Wine, I think, depends almost more on your pocket than on your taste. There's no point in my suggesting a good claret if you can only afford a bottle that's too young to drink. So if your bank balance, like mine, is not what you would like it to be, I would suggest an Entre-deux-Mers for the first two courses to remind you of the summer that has passed. Then go for the best full-bodied red you can afford. For the last two courses, I'd serve a Monbazillac, which I find infinitely more drinkable than fashionable Beaumes de Venise and much cheaper than a good Sauternes.

PINK GRAPEFRUIT GRILLED WITH HONEY

SERVES 6
3 pink grapefruit
3 tablespoons thick honey
ground cinnamon for sprinkling

1. Cut the grapefruit in half then, to make them stand up easily, cut a thin slice off the bottom of each. Cut round each half, loosening the flesh from the outer skin. Cut between the segments to loosen the flesh from the membranes.
2. Spread 2 teaspoons of honey on each grapefruit half and place under a hot grill for 6-7 minutes. Sprinkle with a little cinnamon.

SCALLOPS CHINOISE

If your friends, like mine, are Philistines, and want a cigarette between courses, have the steamer ready over boiling water and put the scallops in when you've served the grapefruit. For a light first course, one scallop per person is sufficient as they are quite rich.

SERVES 6
6 large scallops on their shells
1 tablespoon sesame oil
4 spring onions, trimmed and cut into julienne strips
1 garlic clove
2 tablespoons oyster sauce
2 teaspoons dark soy sauce

1. Steam the scallops for 6-8 minutes, taking care not to overcook them. If you're not ready but the scallops are, turn the heat off and lift the lid slightly. You've got a good 10 minutes leeway then.
2. Heat the sesame oil in a small frying pan and add the spring onions and garlic. Stir quickly and do not allow to colour. Add the oyster and soy sauces and bring to the boil.
3. Place a scallop shell on each plate and spoon over just enough sauce to cover. Serve immediately.

Note:
Ask the fishmonger to clean the scallops but to leave them attached to the shell as evidence of their freshness.

COUNTDOWN

The day before
• *Prepare the autumn fruit salad.*

Three hours before
• *Start roasting the pheasants and make the stock for the sauce.*

One hour before serving
• *Make the croûtes and sauté the mushrooms for the pheasant dish.*
• *Prepare the salad and dressing if wanted.*
• *Prepare the spring onions in julienne strips and chop the garlic for the scallops.*
• *Cut the grapefruit in half and spread with the honey.*

Half an hour before serving
• *Heat the grill.*
• *Set the steamer over a pan of water and bring to boil.*
• *Strain the sauce for poaching the pheasant breasts into a shallow pan.*

PHEASANT IN PORT SAUCE

Ask the butcher for the youngest hen pheasants available, preferably hung for 4-5 days. Guinea hens could be substituted.

SERVES 6

about 200g/7oz butter
3 hen pheasants
strips of fat bacon for barding
1 large marrow bone or calf's foot
1 onion
1 head garlic, unpeeled
3 small leeks
3 celery stalks
3 carrots
2-3 dried mushrooms or mushroom trimmings
piece of orange peel
1 bay leaf
handful of fresh mixed herbs
½ bottle port, plus extra
6 slices of bread, crusts off
1 teaspoon redcurrant jelly
1 teaspoon cornflour
250g/8oz wild mushrooms
watercress to garnish

1. Heat the oven to 200C/400F/gas 6. Put a knob of butter inside each bird and truss them. Bard them with strips of fat bacon. Roast for 25-30 minutes, according to the size of the birds, basting occasionally. Remove the trussing strings and let the pheasants cool for a few minutes. Carefully remove the breast fillets; cover but do not put them in the refrigerator.

2. Deglaze the roasting pan with a little water and put the juices in a large saucepan. Chop the carcasses roughly, including the legs, and add to the pan with the split marrow bone or calf's foot. Add enough cold water to cover and bring to the boil. As the stock approaches boiling point, turn it down to a slow simmer and skim it carefully. When you have more or less cleared the initial scum, add all the vegetables for the stock except the wild mushrooms. Add the orange peel and herbs. Con-

tinue to simmer and skim for 1½ hours, when the stock will have reduced.

3. Strain the stock into a clean pan and return the marrow bone or calf's foot to the stock. Add the port and boil to reduce to about 850ml/1½pt stock – it should be slightly syrupy and almost clear.

4. While the stock is reducing, fry the slices of bread for the croûtes in 100g/4oz butter until they are just golden; drain on absorbent paper and keep them warm in a low oven. Sauté the wild mushrooms in 50g/2oz butter and keep them warm. Stir the redcurrant jelly into the sauce. Mix the corn-

CHICORY 'MOUSSE'

This is not really a mousse, but the name is justified by the fluffy texture. What's more, it sounds better than baked chicory.

SERVES 6

250g/8oz butter
juice of 1 lemon
12 tight heads of chicory
2 teaspoons soft brown sugar
salt and freshly ground pepper
freshly grated nutmeg
200ml/7fl. oz double cream
chopped fresh parsley to garnish (optional)

1. Melt the butter in a pan that will hold nearly all the chicory in one layer (they shrink slightly during cooking). Add the lemon juice and bring to the boil; add the chicory. When the butter comes back to the boil, turn the heat down and cover the pan with greaseproof paper. Put the lid on and simmer for 10 minutes.

2. Remove the lid and greaseproof paper. Turn the chicory and sprinkle with sugar, a little salt and pepper, and nutmeg. Replace the paper and lid and poach slowly for another 30 minutes, checking and turning the chicory every 10 minutes. Don't overheat.

3. Lift the chicory from the butter with a slotted spoon to drain. Remove excess butter with a paper towel. Place the chicory in a gratin dish, in one layer. Grate a little more nutmeg over, then pour the cream over, trying to cover all the chicory. Cover with greaseproof paper and keep in a low oven until needed. The cream should have all but disappeared when the chicory is served – after about an hour. Sprinkle with chopped parsley, if you wish.

Note:

There is sometimes confusion between chicory and endive. The small, tight, pale greeny-yellow heads (called for in this dish) and known as chicory in England, are called *endive* in France.

flour with a tablespoon of port and add to the sauce; heat gently to thicken, then add any juices from the mushrooms.

5. If the pheasant breasts are raw on the inside, seal them for a minute in the remaining butter, then reheat in the sauce, without boiling. If the breasts are almost cooked, poach them in the sauce for about 5 minutes in order to reheat them.

6. Place each breast on a croûte, pour over a little of the sauce and garnish with the watercress. Serve accompanied by the wild mushrooms and the chicory mousse (see following recipe).

WINE NOTES

Entre-deux-Mers, a big tongue of land between Bordeaux's two rivers, used to be known for medium-sweet and dull white wine. These days it is mostly dry, but still apt to be boring. So do not accept just any Entre-deux-Mers. Really sappy, stylish and refreshing Sauvignon-dominated wines come from Châteaux Moulin-de-Launay, Launay, Bonnet and Fongrave.

Certainly there is no need to pay a fortune for fine red wine to go with the pheasant. Some fine wines are astonishingly cheap, notably those from Portugal, a favourite source for full-bodied reds of real character. J. M. da Fonseca wines are outstanding, but look out also for Garrafeira (specially selected) wines, Tinto da Anfora, or mature wines from Bairrada.

To support Harvey Sambrook's contention about Monbazillac, I would recommend wines from Châteaux Treuil-de-Nailhac, Le Fage, Septy or Monbazillac.

AUTUMN FRUIT SALAD IN WINE

SERVES 6

6 small hard pears (preferably Comice)
2 thin-skinned, sweet oranges, well scrubbed
12 dried prunes
12 walnuts
1 bay leaf
1 small cinnamon stick
1 vanilla pod
2 cloves
100g/4oz soft brown sugar
1 bottle full-bodied red wine
mint sprigs to garnish
cream to serve

1. Peel the pears but leave the stalks on. Cut the oranges into 5mm/¼in slices, discarding the end slices. Arrange the pears so that they stand upright in a pan. Add the prunes, walnuts, bay leaf, cinnamon, vanilla, cloves and sugar, and put the orange slices on top. Pour in the wine, topping up with water, if necessary, to just cover the fruit. Poach gently for 20-30 minutes, until just tender. Leave to cool.

2. Remove the fruit and arrange it equally in 6 individual dishes. Discard the cinnamon stick, vanilla pod, bay leaf and cloves. If the syrup is too thin, boil it down to about 6 tablespoons. Cool, then pour over the fruit. Garnish with mint; serve cold with cream.

Glynn Christian

GOLDEN AUTUMN MENU

Transform a gloomy evening into a sparkling occasion with Glynn Christian's menu inspired by gold and precious gems

Deep-sea caskets with pearls and prawns

Baby turkey breasts in a cranberry and pecan overcoat
Souffléed pumpkin with allspice

Coconut and chocolate truffle loaf with nuggets of pineapple

Gold, jewels and treasures have fascinated me ever since I could read adventure stories in the *Boy's Own Paper* and see Arabian Nights-style adventures at the Saturday cinema. I still love the idea of times when displays of jewelled magnificence helped emperors rule the world – it's Tutankhamen's fabulous treasures that are remembered, not his reign.

The Great Moguls lived with unimaginable fortunes swagged about them. Their collections of precious stones and beads, pearls, rubies, lapis, gold and silver were stored in caskets and its was with thoughts of those that I planned the first dish in my menu; a casket crammed with the buried treasures of the oceans. The selection of vegetables looks like precious stones (I've never been able to resist the magical effect that blanching has on cucumber, turning it into the most stunning jade). The inclusion of prawns suggests strands

of coral, leek cream has a foamy sea-greenness and dill has an affinity with all things fishy. And what else but a crisp golden-coloured casket in which to present them? I love the crunch of pastry to start a meal.

I turned to the New World for the main course, for I am entranced with the Inca and Aztec and their gold on one hand, and with the extraordinary culinary treasures with which the old world enriched the new on the other. Thus the main course is very much a celebration of the produce originally developed and grown by the old civilizations of North and South America. I've added gin and mint to give necessary sharpness to the turkey, which will be appreciated as a contrast to the sweetness of American vegetables.

Turkey with a cranberry and pecan overcoat is planned so the fiddly bits are done in advance. It

shows how it is possible to get the best results and true flavours without time-wasting techniques that cannot be tasted. One of my strongest rules in planning a recipe is if you can't taste it, don't put it in or don't do it!

With the turkey you can choose any of the New World vegetables, but I would keep them simple and go towards the sweeter ones, to complement the slightly astringent flavour of the turkey and cranberry sauce. I suggest souffléed pumpkin with allspice, and green beans, either plain or tossed in garlic butter. But other options are wild rice pilaf; baby sweetcorn in garlic

COUNTDOWN

The day before
• *Bake the pastry caskets and store in an airtight tin.*
• *Make the truffle loaf and refrigerate in its mould.*

In the morning
• *Remove breasts from turkey and marinate in gin for 4 hours. Remove dark meat from carcass and make the cranberry overcoat. Prepare the golden turkey stock, allowing about 3 hours for cooking.*
• *Prepare vegetables and prawns for filling, store covered in the refrigerator.*
• *Cook leek cream, cover and chill.*
• *Make dillweed and pepper-flavoured vodka.*
• *Cook pasta shells.*

Three hours before
• *Coat and shape the breasts with the cranberry mixture and leave at room temperature.*
• *Make cranberry sauce and strain.*
• *Make pumpkin purée.*
• *Top and tail the green beans.*

One hour before
• *Unmould the truffle loaf and slice thinly. Prepare extra fresh pineapple and sprinkle with rum and vanilla. If using, whip cream, flavour and chill.*
• *Put pudding plates in refrigerator.*
• *Heat oven to 180C/350F/gas 4 and bake turkey breasts, allowing an extra ¼ hour for standing time.* ▶

butter, with a scattering of diced capsicum; green beans with wild rice; mashed potatoes or mashed sweet potatoes; steamed strips of mixed green and red peppers; baked stuffed tomatoes.

The meal ends with coconut and chocolate truffle loaf studded with nuggets of fresh pineapple. Its rich flavour is balanced by the slight sharpness of the pineapple. It looks better for being prepared well in advance.

My menu celebrates gold and jewels, but it is also planned to let you celebrate, for most of the work is done in advance. With Christmas on the way, turkey in an overcoat might be the key to letting you join the festivities, too.

DEEP-SEA CASKETS WITH PEARLS AND PRAWNS

Pearls and jade were coveted far more than diamonds at one time. Here, they are hidden in a painted casket of puff pastry, which sits upon a sea-green sauce decorated with green or white pasta shells.

SERVES 6

400g/14oz made-weight puff pastry, fresh or frozen
yellow food colouring or saffron powder and 1 egg yolk, beaten
1 egg, beaten
1 cucumber
3 fat courgettes
175g/6oz mooli (daikon or Japanese radish)
250g/8oz peeled, cooked prawns, defrosted slowly if frozen
18 small pasta shells, green or white
350g/12oz leeks, thinly sliced including most of green part
300ml/½pt double cream
salt and pepper
6 tablespoons vodka
1 heaped tablespoon dried dillweed
6 crushed black peppercorns
50g/2oz butter, cut in small pieces
fresh dill or herbs to garnish

1. Roll out the pastry evenly to an oblong about 27.5cm × 15cm/9in × 6in. Cut into 6 pieces about 8cm/3in square and transfer to a baking sheet. With a very sharp knife-blade knock up the edges all round to encourage the pastry to rise more, then scallop them.

2. Paint the tops of the caskets with undiluted food colouring. Put them into the refrigerator for about 20 minutes until the colouring is really dry. Meanwhile heat the oven to 220C/425F/gas 7. Then paint the pastry again with beaten egg to glaze. (If you object to food colouring, mix saffron powder with a beaten egg yolk and paint the pastry with this.)

3. Put the caskets into the oven and immediately reduce the temperature to 200C/400F/gas 6. Bake for about 25 minutes until they are well risen and the sides are golden.

4. Allow to cool for a few moments then slice off the 'lid' to allow steam to escape and the pastry to crisp. Once cool, cut around with a sharp knife and then remove every bit of damp and uncooked pastry from inside the casket to make a crisp shell.

5. Peel the cucumber and reserve the skin. Using the smallest size melon-ball cutter, prepare 30 balls of cucumber. Peel the courgettes and the mooli; cut 30 balls from each of these, too.

6. Plunge the vegetable balls into boiling water for 2-3 minutes then leave under running cold water until cold. The cucumber should look like jade and the mooli and courgette like coloured pearls. Mix the vegetable balls with the prawns and set aside.

7. Cook the pasta shells as directed on packet and reserve.

8. Cook the leeks with the cucumber skin in a heavy saucepan, stirring constantly and adding no extra liquid or fat. In 5 minutes they should be soft, but still retain an intense colour. Tip into a food processor and purée while slowly adding the cream. Process for a minute, then push through a fine sieve. Season lightly with salt and pepper. The dish can be prepared ahead up to this point.

9. Mix together the vodka, dillweed

Ten minutes before

• *Reheat the pastry caskets in the bottom of the oven. Warm the leek cream. Melt the butter and add the strained vodka. Add the prawns and vegetables and heat gently. Add pasta shells to leek cream.*

• *Warm plates for the first course.*

• *Fold the egg whites into the pumpkin and bake for 20-30 minutes.*

• *Just before the meal, remove turkey from the oven.*

• *Warm plates for main course.*

• *Put water for cooking beans over a low heat.*

• *Ladle leek cream around caskets and garnish. Serve at once.*

After the first course

• *Warm the cranberry sauce and complete with the gin, seasoning and butter.*

• *Cook the green beans for a few minutes, drain, and toss in garlic butter if using.*

• *Cut souffléed pumpkin into segments.*

• *Slice the turkey at the table.*

After the main course

• *Arrange the sliced truffle loaf on individual chilled plates, garnish and serve.*

and black peppercorns, and heat, co-vered, for 3 minutes, but do not allow to boil. Leave covered until ready to serve.
10. When you are ready to eat, warm 6 dinner plates and gently heat the pastry caskets in the bottom of the oven.
11. Melt the butter over low heat in a wide-bottomed saucepan – a tall narrow one means you will take too long to heat the ingredients and some will lose their liquid. Strain in the dillweed and pep-per-flavoured vodka using a small tea strainer. Once the mixture is hot, tip in

the vegetables and prawns, and leave over gentle heat for a few minutes until warmed through. At the same time, reheat the leek cream.
12. Drop the pasta shells into the hot leek cream to warm through. Put the bases of the caskets on the warm plates and fill just to the top with the vegetable and prawn mixture. Dribble in the hot vodka butter. Place the lids on top.
13. Arrange 3 hot pasta shells on each plate, then ladle the leek cream around each casket. Decorate with fresh dill.

BABY TURKEY BREASTS IN A CRANBERRY AND PECAN OVERCOAT

A celebration of the New World's culinary treasures, this is perfect special-occasion food. The hard work is done in advance and the carving is simple.

SERVES 6

1 fresh or frozen dressed baby turkey with giblets, weighing about 3kg/6½lb
8 tablespoons gin
100g/4oz chopped onion
1 bay leaf
1 celery stalk
1 sprig of thyme
1L/2pt boiling water
1 garlic clove
100g/4oz fresh wholemeal bread
250g/8oz fresh or frozen cranberries
2 teaspoons dried mint
salt
50g/2oz (or more) pecans
pepper
50g/2oz cold diced butter, to finish the sauce

1. Remove the turkey's giblets, pull off and discard the skin. With a very sharp knife remove both sides of breast meat in single pieces. This is very simple to do if you start by cutting down either side of the thin breast keel and then cut around the rib cage with the blade of the knife angled in towards the bone.

2. Trim the breasts neatly and put them into a shallow flat dish. Pour 6 tablespoons of gin over and cover. Leave at room temperature for 4 hours, basting and turning occasionally.

3. Remove all the dark meat from the carcass, legs and wings and put to one side with the heart and liver. Chop up the carcass and brown it well, together with the gizzard and chopped neck, in a heavy saucepan. Add 50g/2oz onion, the bay leaf, celery and thyme and pour on the boiling water. Cook gently for 4-5 hours, strain then return to the pan and reduce until you have 300ml/½pt of rich golden turkey stock.

4. Purée the remaining onion with the garlic. Purée the dark turkey meat, liver and heart (not the breasts) separately – it is better from the point of view of texture to process half the meat finely and the rest coarsely.

5. Make the wholemeal breadcrumbs in the blender, add 100g/4oz cranberries and chop, but do not reduce them to a purée. Add the bread and cranberry mixture to the onion, garlic and puréed turkey. Sprinkle with mint and pour in gin marinade from the turkey. Knead and squeeze everything together with your hands until it is all thoroughly mixed, and removing any remaining sinews.

6. Divide the mixture into 2 on a baking tray or in a shallow roasting pan. Squash the 2 portions out until there is a hollow equivalent to the size of a turkey breast in the middle of each; the mixture should be about 5mm/¼in thick. Salt the turkey breasts very lightly and cover each breast completely with the mixture, making sure it is not too thick over the tip of the breast. Smooth the surface and twist the narrow end of the coating to make each shape like a thick comma.

7. Press pecan halves into the mixture: 50g/2oz is enough for an undivided line down the centre of each, but if you have more you can make whatever pattern you like. The dish can be prepared ahead up to this stage.

8. Leave the patterned breasts in a cool place, but not the refrigerator, for at least an hour.

9. You can also make the sauce in advance. Heat 300ml/½pt rich turkey stock and tip in the remaining cranberries. Cook just until the cranberries are popping, then liquidize and press the berries through a fine sieve.

10. Bring the breasts to room temperature before cooking them. Heat the oven to 180C/350F/gas 4. Cook the breasts for about 1 hour, allowing an extra 15 minutes' standing time.

11. When you are ready to serve, reheat the sauce to simmering, then remove from heat. Stir in the remaining 2 tablespoons of gin and about ½ teaspoon salt and a little freshly ground pepper, then lightly stir in the butter in 4 batches, adding each one just before the last piece melts.

SOUFFLÉED PUMPKIN WITH ALLSPICE

Pumpkins are enormously varied in texture, sweetness and moisture content. Among the firmest are the grey-skinned Queensland Blue and the gourd-shaped Butternut, but you can use whatever type you find. Allspice was so named because it tastes like a combination of all the sweet spices.

SERVES 6

1kg/2lb chopped pumpkin
50g/2oz butter, plus extra for greasing
salt and white pepper
½ teaspoon ground allspice
3 eggs

1. Cook the pumpkin in lightly salted water until tender. Drain, then return to the saucepan over low heat and bash the pumpkin around a little to let it dry, as when making mashed potatoes. It should be quite thick and look rather waxy. Heat the oven to 180C/350F/gas 4.

2. Tip into a blender, add the butter, salt, pepper, most of the allspice, 1 whole egg and 2 egg yolks, and purée. Taste and adjust the allspice, salt and pepper. This can be done in advance and the purée can then be gently reheated when you are ready to continue.

3. Whisk 2 egg whites until stiff. Stir a quarter of the whisked egg whites into the pumpkin purée to lighten it and then fold in the rest.

4. Ladle into a buttered 23cm/9in pie dish and bake for 20-30 minutes until risen and lightly browned on top. Allow to settle for at least 5 minutes before cutting into segments. It may crumple a little, but I think this looks rather more welcoming than something too tailor-made.

Note:

If your oven cannot handle the turkey and the soufflé together, simply serve this dish as a purée.

WINE NOTES

If you would like an aperitif which would also suit the first course, a Manzanilla sherry would be a good choice. The word means 'little green apple' so you can tell that the wine is supposed to have a fresh acidic bite. Manzanillas are matured by the sea at Sanlucar, and there is said to be a tang of sea-salt, reminiscent of the Spanish Main, about their nose and flavour. Barbadillo are leading producers, and it is a good idea to seek out wines bottled in Spain for that extra freshness vital to the wine's proper enjoyment. It needs to be drunk like white wine: well chilled, and ideally at a single sitting.

To go with the main course, choose one of the modern treasures of the New World: Zinfandel, the fruity, brambly wine made from the grape variety that is exclusively grown in California is ideal. Fetzer is a popular brand, Louis Martini and Paul Masson good and inexpensive, Heitz dependably good, and Ridge vineyards outstanding.

For the dessert wine, late-picked Muscat from Australia makes a more intense and fragrant alternative to the now familiar Muscat de Beaumes de Venise. Brown Bros. wines are reliable, and now quite widely available.

COCONUT AND CHOCOLATE TRUFFLE LOAF WITH NUGGETS OF PINEAPPLE

This exotic cake is lighter than you might expect and needs no baking. It may be presented as simply or as dramatically as you choose. Try to use fresh rather than canned pineapple for the enticing contrast of sharp and sweet.

SERVES 6

350g/12oz fresh, trimmed pineapple
4 tablespoons dark rum
1 teaspoon vanilla essence
200g/7oz plain chocolate
175g/6oz creamed coconut
100g/4oz unsalted butter
200g/7oz packet gingernut biscuits
oil for greasing
extra pineapple and pineapple leaves to decorate
double cream (optional) to serve

1. Chop the pineapple into small chunks, then marinate them in the rum and vanilla extract for a couple of hours.
2. Melt together the chocolate, creamed coconut and butter over gentle heat. Crush the gingernut biscuits finely and stir evenly into the warm mixture. Mix in the marinade from the pineapple, then stir in the pineapple.
3. Lightly oil a 1.5L/2½pt loaf tin and line the base with greaseproof or waxed paper. Pile in the mixture and press down lightly to ensure it is even. Cover and chill overnight at least. Unmould and slice thinly.
4. Serve very cold and decorate with a little more pineapple, sprinkled with rum and vanilla. If you want to serve it with cream, whip it lightly and stir in a little pineapple juice and/or rum.

Note:
Creamed coconut is available in solid blocks from supermarkets and Indian grocers.

Sonia Blech

FRENCH POLISH

When Christmas – and all its largesse – is just around the corner, prepare yourself with Sonia Blech's sophisticated but light and healthy menu

---

Carrot and avocado mosaic with yellow pepper coulis

Broccoli moulds with scallops and prawns

Parcels of halibut and salmon dressed in green

Citrus fruit with sabayon brûlée

COUNTDOWN

In the morning
• *Prepare the terrine and the coulis and chill.*
• *Prepare the fish parcels and accompanying vegetables, cover and chill them.*

Two hours before
• *Boil the stock for the moulds and leave to cool.*
• *Prepare the fruit in wine.*

One hour before
• *Prepare the broccoli moulds and make the sauce.*

Just before
• *Remove the terrine from the refrigerator.*
• *Heat the oven.*

During the first course
• *Cook the broccoli moulds and reheat the sauce.*

During the second course
• *Steam the fish parcels over the accompanying vegetables.*

After the third course
• *Make the sabayon sauce and finish the dessert.*

What makes cooking such a wonderful occupation is its universal appeal. You don't by any means need to be a professional to succeed, but you do need sensitivity, flair, intelligence and love. Love of food is not gluttony; it generates the same pleasure, the same *joie de vivre* as the love of music or paintings or any other artistic expression. Cooking also requires respect for the ingredients one is using, as well as respect for the people for whom one is cooking. One must also realize that taste in food is not 'absolute', just as the criteria of beauty are not absolute. As many faces as there are in the world, are there different palates!

With this in mind, I always cook things that I love, the way I love them, but am always prepared to adapt to the particular needs of a customer if I can, as it is his or her enjoyment, ultimately, that matters. Here I have tried to create a menu that is rich in feel but light and delicate on the digestion. I feel that everything we eat should benefit not only the soul but also the body. But healthy eating does not mean ascetism, soya beans, vegetable juices and pulses ad infinitum. It means the right balance of all things, including dairy produce, meats, sweets, etc. to give you health, happiness and — I hope — the joy of good food.

CARROT AND AVOCADO MOSAIC WITH YELLOW PEPPER COULIS

Mosaïque de carottes et d'avocats au coulis de poivrons jaunes

SERVES 8

11 leaves gelatine or 4×11g sachets powdered gelatine
1L/2pt fresh carrot juice (or bottled carrot juice from health food shops)
juice of 1½ oranges
sprig of tarragon
juice of ⅓ lemon
2 large, ripe avocado pears
red pepper, cut into diamonds, and tarragon sprigs, to garnish
FOR THE COULIS
2 yellow peppers, coarsely chopped
juice of ½ orange
sprig of tarragon
pinch of salt

1. Soak 10 of the gelatine leaves in cold water to cover, until soft. Soak the remaining leaf separately in cold water. Alternatively, reserve 1 teaspoon of the powdered gelatine and sprinkle the rest over 300ml/½pt of the carrot juice and leave until spongy. Sprinkle the reserved teaspoon of gelatine over 2 tablespoons water and leave until spongy.

2. Put the remaining carrot juice and the juice of 1 orange into a pan and add the tarragon. Bring to the boil, skim, and remove from the heat. Add the larger quantity of gelatine, stir to dissolve; leave until cool but not set. Remove the tarragon sprig.

3. Heat the remaining orange juice with the lemon juice. Bring to the boil and remove from the heat. Add the remaining softened gelatine and stir to dissolve.

From left: carrot and avocado mosaic with yellow pepper coulis; broccoli moulds with scallops and prawns; parcels of halibut and salmon dressed in green; and (background) citrus fruit with sabayon brûlée

4. Peel the avocados and put one and a half in a liquidizer with the citrus juices and gelatine. Blend until smooth. Transfer to a dish and add the remaining avocado half, cut into tiny cubes. Put this mixture into a piping bag, fitted with a 1cm/½in plain nozzle.

5. Pour a 1cm/½in-deep layer of carrot liquid into the terrine and put into the freezer until set. Remove and pipe 3 bands of avocado on to the jelly, along the length of the terrine, starting 1cm/½in from each edge and leaving 1.5cm/¾in between the rows. Cover with carrot liquid and return to the freezer until set.

6. Pipe another 2 bands on top of the set jelly, to lie between the first 3 bands. Cover with the carrot jelly and return to the freezer. Carry on until all the avocado has been used up, finishing with a 5mm/¼in layer of jelly. Freeze only until completely set. The terrine can be kept in a very cold refrigerator for up to 8 hours.

7. Make the coulis. Put the peppers in a pan with the orange juice and add water to cover. Add the tarragon and salt and cook until very soft. Blend in a liquidizer until smooth, then strain. Chill.

8. To serve, unmould the chilled terrine, and slice. Spoon a little coulis on to individual plates and place a slice of terrine on top. Garnish with pepper and tarragon.

BROCCOLI MOULDS WITH SCALLOPS AND PRAWNS
Chartreuses de broccolis aux coquilles St Jacques et crevettes

For this dish you need eight 7cm/3in diameter × 4cm/1½in deep individual moulds – similar in shape to Christmas pudding basins.

SERVES 8

1.5L/2½pt home-made stock (chicken, fish or vegetable)
3 stalks lemon grass, finely chopped
salt
700g/1½lb broccoli
350g/12oz unpeeled prawns, plus extra to garnish
14 scallops
flat-leaved parsley to garnish
FOR THE SAUCE
dash of olive oil
1 stalk lemon grass, chopped
1 garlic clove, green centre removed
5 tomatoes, chopped
juice of 1 small orange
1 julienne strip orange zest

1. Bring the stock to the boil and add the lemon grass. Remove from the heat and leave until cold. Meanwhile, bring a large pan of slightly salted water to the boil and add the broccoli. Cook until tender but still firm to the bite. Strain and cool immediately in very cold water.

2. Pour half the cooled stock into a bowl. Chop the broccoli by hand very, very finely and add to the stock in the bowl.

3. Peel the prawns, reserving the shells and heads for the sauce. Separate the corals from the scallops and reserve them for the sauce.

4. Bring the remaining stock to the boil once again, drop in the scallops and cook for 1 minute. Add the prawns and immediately strain the whole lot, reserving the stock as well.

5. Slice the scallops horizontally into discs the thickness of a pound coin. Reserve the 8 best discs and halve the rest. Halve the prawns, lengthways.

Strain the broccoli thoroughly, reserving the stock.

6. Place one of the scallop discs in the base of each mould and line the sides with a layer of halved scallop slices and halved prawns.

7. Spoon the strained broccoli into the centre up to the level of the prawns. Arrange another ring of seafood around the sides, on a brick-laying principle, then fill the centre with more broccoli. Continue until the moulds are full, then press down on each one very hard to pack the contents together and extract the excess liquid.

8. Make the sauce. Heat the oil in a non-stick pan and when very hot add the prawn shells, the corals from the scallops, lemon grass, garlic and tomatoes. Add all the reserved stock, the orange juice and julienne strip of orange zest. Bring to the boil, then remove the julienne strip and liquidize the mixture. Strain very thoroughly and check seasoning.

9. Heat the oven to 180C/350F/gas 4. Put the moulds into a roasting tin half-filled with water, and cover loosely with foil. Cook for 15 minutes until the contents are thoroughly heated.

10. To serve, unmould on to individual plates and pour a little sauce around each one. Garnish each plate with some parsley and a shelled prawn.

Note:
Fresh lemon grass can be bought at Waitrose and also at Chinese supermarkets.

PARCELS OF HALIBUT AND SALMON DRESSED IN GREEN
Paupiettes de flétan et de saumon en habit vert

SERVES 8

700g/1½lb fillet of halibut, skinned
500g/1lb fillet of salmon, skinned
2 heads Chinese leaves
salt and freshly ground black pepper
4 tablespoons snipped chives, plus extra to garnish
8 round radishes
5 small-medium carrots
600ml/1pt bottled mineral water
sprig of fresh basil
sprig of fresh tarragon
1 julienne strip lemon rind
600ml/1pt home-made fish or vegetable stock

1. With a very sharp filleting knife, cut each fillet horizontally into 4 very thin slices, as if you were cutting smoked salmon, then halve each slice.

2. Pull off the largest Chinese leaves and cut away the hard central ribs, keeping the leaves as whole as possible. Put them into a basin and pour boiling water over; remove immediately and refresh with cold running water until completely cold. Pat dry and then cut into strips the same size as the fish.

3. Lay a strip of leaf on the worktop and place a strip of halibut on top. Sprinkle with salt, pepper and chives. Lay another strip of leaf on top, then a strip of salmon; season and add chives. Finally roll the pile up and trim the ends. Make 7 more rolls in the same way. Patch any uncovered pieces of fish with Chinese leaves. If you like, you can place the rolls on a plate covered with absorbent paper and chill for up to 8 hours.

4. With a canelle knife make 5 incisions from top to bottom around each radish and carrot. Slice thinly.

5. Put the mineral water, basil, tarragon, lemon rind and stock into the base of a steamer. Bring to the boil, and add the carrot slices.

6. Arrange the fish parcels in the steamer basket, place the basket over the pan, and cook for 12-14 minutes. Take off the heat and add the radishes to the stock. Allow to rest for 5 minutes. Then remove the *paupiettes*. Slice each one. Strain the stock.

7. To serve, spoon a pool of the stock on to 8 individual plates and arrange a sliced *paupiette* on each. Garnish with carrots, radishes and chives and serve with a lightly steamed vegetable.

CITRUS FRUIT WITH SABAYON BRÛLÉE
Gratin des agrumes au zabayon de Beaumes de Venise

SERVES 8

1 small pineapple
3 very large oranges
2 pink grapefruit
2 ugli fruit
3 jaffarenes
1 bottle Muscat de Beaumes de Venise
8 egg yolks

1. Peel and core the pineapple and cut the flesh into thin semi-circles. (Reserve the leaves for garnish.) Peel all the citrus fruit and separate into skinless segments by cutting down on either side of each membrane with a very sharp knife. You can cut the grapefruit slices into quarters if you prefer. Combine all the fruit flesh in a bowl and pour in half the wine.

2. Set a heatproof glass mixing bowl over boiling water. When very hot, add the egg yolks and a tablespoon of water and whisk thoroughly until white, fluffy and voluminous.

3. Meanwhile, bring the remaining wine to the boil. Pour over the egg yolks, still whisking. Transfer the mixture to a saucepan and whisk over a gentle heat until almost boiling.

4. Just before serving, heat the grill and put the fruit and juice into a gratin dish. Pour the sabayon sauce over and place under the very hot grill until glazed, watching constantly. Serve at once, garnished with a few pineapple leaves.

WINE NOTES

Sonia Blech's preferences are for simple but distinctive flavours, and her recipes provide a foil for a mini-parade of starry French white wines. For the mosaïque, *a mild and mellow-flavoured Gewürztraminer, or Muscat d'Alsace, will probably suit better than the more acidic Riesling, but a third Alsatian possibility is Pinot Blanc, an exceptionally versatile and useful food wine—which is still excellent value for money.*

With the chartreuses, *I would turn to direct and deliciously pungent Sauvignon—Sancerre or Pouilly Fumé are the classic appellations, though Sauvignon de St Bris is also excellent—and for the* paupiettes *a Chardonnay, which means the best white burgundy you can buy.*

And with the gratin, *a glass of well-chilled Muscat de Beaumes de Venise will not prove* de trop.

119

WINTER

*W*inter is the time for the earth to rest, for wild animals to hibernate, and for humans to make merry behind closed doors, in front of blazing fires. Bonnie Rabert dispels winter gloom with a cosy all-day brunch: nuts in a warming spicy glaze and a piquant ham and cheese *strata* ('layer-cake') precede spinach-and-mushroom-stuffed chicken thighs, hotted up with a chilli-spiked sauce. Ann Long pampers her guests with one of winter's great luxuries – venison, richly served in puff pastry with a dark plum sauce. Bright green broccoli florets and the sweetest of root vegetables, parsnips (all the better for a touch of frost), prove winter, too, has its bounty.

Broccoli partners the creamy curds of cauliflower and a wonderful fruit-stuffed goose with cranberry and orange sauce in Caroline Waldegrave's Christmas menu. Her idea of a vanilla bombe, secretly concealing macerated prunes, gives an unusually light – though still wickedly delicious – finish to the traditional meal. For vegetarians, Christmas dinner can be a dull affair – but not if you follow Shehzad Husain's lead into the Indian kitchen. More than most does Indian cuisine not only provide vegetarians with a myriad of exotic flavours but it lends itself, too, to festive decoration: silver and gold leaf often adorns dishes both sweet and savoury.

When January's drear days seem interminably long, celebrate the Chinese New Year with Ken Hom. Fried aubergines with a tomato salsa enlivened with ginger (traditionally one of the 'warm' spices), and roasted poussins with a sauce of fiery rice wine are surely the best antidote to bitter winter winds. Soon spring will be on the way: buds miniscule in February will be fat and swollen by March. Instinctively, one looks to brighter days – and lighter meals. Get in trim with Colin Spencer's gourmet vegetarian menu: a delicious sage, celery and dill seed bread – foretaste of all the herbs to come; delicate smoked tofu kebabs and a brightly green gratin of broccoli, courgettes, leeks, avocado and parsley. Spring is almost here . . .

Bonnie Rabert

A WINTER BRUNCH

Not quite breakfast, almost lunch; brunch is a wonderfully informal way of entertaining – Bonnie Rabert suggests highlighting the casual air by serving this menu as a buffet

---

Spicy glazed nuts

Ham and cheese strata

Chicken rolls

Crudités

Sultana rosemary buns

Fruit salad vinaigrette

As a professional cook, I have friends who sometimes feel reluctant or too intimidated to invite me to dine. However, I must admit that I, too, feel nervous when guests share a meal with us; they may expect perfection, but I am only human! For this reason, brunch is the perfect entertaining solution, providing a relaxed atmosphere both for me as hostess, and for our guests.

Brunch is a preplanned breakfast served almost at lunchtime – hence the name. An American institution, it replaces Sunday lunch and often supper, too, depending on the size and richness of the menu. At home in Chicago, it can be served in anticipation of a major American football game; and it makes a most enjoyable way of passing the grey and cold winter weekends, when food, drink and friends provide the warmth we need so badly.

This menu includes several favourites. Strata is popular because it can be assembled the day before the meal and uses up day-old bread instead of making breadcrumbs. Please use one of the good-quality, firm white breads available here, not that spongy stuff.

Several of the dishes combine two or more ingredients where you might use just one. This is not to make the recipes more elaborate, and I hope it will not put you off. I really feel that a combination of cheeses in the strata; dry and fresh mushrooms in the spinach filling; and fresh tomatoes as well as purée in the sauce for the chicken, all add to the flavour. If you're short of time or can't get all the necessary ingredients, you can simplify or make your own substitutions.

I had originally intended the chicken recipe included here to be a pasta dish, but on reflection, there seemed to be too much stodge in the whole menu. So enjoy the chicken rolls with just the sauce this time, and serve it with pasta on another occasion. This brings to mind a few points about planning a menu. Always choose a variety of colours, textures and ingredients. Balancing textures and colours gives a menu that is pleasing to see as well as eat, important because we eat with our eyes first. My husband and I recently attended a pot luck dinner with garlic in every course; and I was once dangerously close to serving an 'all red' meal. Combine tried-

and-trusted recipes with a few new ideas, if that makes you more comfortable. Or serve a completely new menu – what are friends for? I have to chuckle when I read of hostesses who try out all their planned party dishes on the family. Who can afford the time and money for a less than appreciative audience?

Another thing, do not put your menu in writing (except for maga-

zine articles). A menu is just an idea of what you hope will make it to the table. You may need to substitute or eliminate at the last minute. For instance, the sultana rosemary buns should be made on the morning of the brunch, but if your mother or best friend calls because you haven't written, you won't be able to get them done. So just in case this sort of thing happens, buy some suitable

alternative buns to have available as a safety net.

To get the proceedings off to a lively start, serve a luscious champagne cocktail made with the French aperitif La Belle Sandrine, a mixture of armagnac and passion fruit juice.

We encourage informality by presenting this casual menu buffet-style. See you on Sunday?

COUNTDOWN

The day before
• *Make spicy glazed nuts and store in an airtight container.*
• *Prepare filling and sauce for the chicken rolls. Refrigerate both overnight.*
• *Layer the ham and cheese strata and chill.*
• *To save time next morning, you could start the sultana rosemary buns and leave the dough in the refrigerator to rise overnight.*

In the morning
• *Take ham and cheese strata and all the ingredients for the chicken rolls out of the refrigerator to bring to room temperature.*
• *If you have not already done so, make sultana rosemary buns and leave to rise for 40-50 minutes.*
• *Stuff, tie up and fry the chicken rolls. Put the sauce, then the chicken, in a baking dish and cover with foil ready to bake.*

One and half hours before brunch
• *Chill the champagne.*
• *Heat the oven to 200C/400F/gas 6.*
• *Prepare crudité vegetables, wash the salad vegetables and prepare fruit for melon salad.*
• *Bake the buns.*
• *Make up the salad dressing so the flavours have time to blend.*
• *Take out buns; reduce oven temperature to 180C/350F/ gas 4.* ▶

SPICY GLAZED NUTS

These tempting appetizers are ideal served with drinks before a meal, and can be made several days in advance.

SERVES 6

75g/3oz granulated sugar
1 teaspoon ground cinnamon
1 teaspoon ground coriander
$\frac{1}{4}$ teaspoon salt
1 large egg white
500g/1lb mixed nuts such as hazelnuts, blanched almonds and pecans
butter for greasing

1. Heat oven to 110C/225F/gas $\frac{1}{4}$. Combine sugar, cinnamon, coriander and salt. In a medium-sized bowl, whisk egg white with 1 teaspoon water until frothy but not stiff.
2. Add mixed nuts to egg-white mixture, stirring to coat evenly. Sprinkle with sugar mixture, tossing lightly with two forks to coat.
3. Spread nuts in a single layer in a large buttered baking tray and bake for about an hour, stirring every 15 minutes. Cool and store in an airtight container until ready to serve.

HAM AND CHEESE STRATA

Similar to a Welsh cheese pudding, this savoury dish combines bread with ham and cheese in a mustardy egg custard. The Italian name *strata* comes from the layering of the ingredients.

SERVES 6

300g/11oz day-old Italian bread or French stick with the crust removed, cut into 5mm/$\frac{1}{4}$in cubes
100g/4oz sliced boiled ham, trimmed of fat and chopped
175g/6oz English Cheddar, coarsely grated
100g/4oz Jarlsberg, Emmenthal or Gruyère cheese, coarsely grated
salt and freshly ground white pepper
25g/1oz butter
3 spring onions, sliced
5 large eggs
600ml/1pt milk
1 rounded tablespoon Dijon mustard

1. Butter an oblong 2L/3$\frac{1}{2}$pt baking dish and line the bottom with half of the bread cubes. Sprinkle with half of the ham and cheeses, seasoning lightly.

2. Sauté sliced spring onions in melted butter until soft. Scatter them over mixture in baking dish. Repeat the layers of bread, ham and cheese.

3. Beat eggs with milk, mustard and a little seasoning. Pour over cheese mixture. Cover with cling film and leave to stand at room temperature for 1-2 hours or overnight in the refrigerator (if chilled, let the dish return to room temperature before baking).

4. Heat the oven to 180C/350F/gas 4. Uncover baking dish, bake until top is golden brown and custard is set, about 40 minutes. Let stand before slicing.

CHICKEN ROLLS

Don't be discouraged by the length of this recipe; the filling and sauce can be made a day ahead. It's worth it.

SERVES 6

12 chicken thighs, skinned and boned
salt and freshly ground black pepper
25g/1oz butter
FOR THE SPINACH MUSHROOM FILLING
20g/$\frac{3}{4}$oz dried porcini *mushrooms*
75g/3oz button mushrooms, thinly sliced, alone or in combination with dried shiitake *mushrooms*
350g/12oz fresh spinach
$\frac{1}{2}$ bunch watercress leaves and tender stems, chopped
25g/1oz butter
100g/4oz cream cheese
25g/1oz Parmesan cheese, freshly grated
salt and freshly ground black pepper
freshly grated nutmeg
FOR THE TOMATO AND CARROT SAUCE
2 tablespoons olive oil
1 shallot, finely chopped
100g/4oz carrots, sliced
1 small garlic clove, crushed
2 large ripe tomatoes, weighing about 500g/1lb in total, peeled, seeded and chopped
1 tablespoon tomato purée
1 whole red chilli, halved and seeded
salt and pepper to taste

1. First, make the spinach mushroom filling. Soak both dried *porcini* and *shiitake* mushrooms (if using) in hot water to cover. Leave for 30 minutes. Drain mushrooms, squeeze dry and chop.

2. Wash spinach thoroughly. Fill a sink or large roasting tin with cold water, let spinach soak in water for a few minutes, then rinse each leaf before discarding stem and draining leaves. Place spinach in large pot with just the water clinging to the leaves. Cover and bring to boil, remove from heat and let stand for 2 minutes until leaves are wilted. Turn from top to bottom once. Drain in colander and squeeze to remove excess moisture. Chop and combine with watercress; set aside.

3. Melt butter in a frying pan and sauté fresh and dried mushrooms until tender. Add spinach mixture, cream cheese and grated Parmesan, stirring well to combine. Remove from heat – season to taste with salt, pepper and nutmeg. Cool, place the filling in a covered container and refrigerate overnight.

4. Now make the tomato and carrot sauce. Heat oil in a saucepan. Sauté shallot, carrots and garlic until shallot is soft. Add tomatoes, tomato purée, chilli, salt and pepper.

Countdown (continued)

An hour before eating

• *Bake ham and cheese strata – it needs to stand for several minutes before being cut.*
• *Arrange the crudités and the fruit salad decoratively on platters.*
• *Prepare buffet table and set out cold dishes.*
• *About 30 minutes before the meal, make up and serve the champagne cocktails.*
• *About 15 minutes before serving, put chicken rolls in the oven to warm through.*

Just before the meal

• *Quickly whisk the vinaigrette dressing with a fork and drizzle over fruit salad.*

Facing page: ham and cheese strata. Below: chicken rolls with tomato and carrot sauce

5. Cover and simmer for 15 minutes. Remove chilli, adjust seasoning and set aside to cool slightly. Purée in food processor. Refrigerate in a covered container overnight.

6. On the morning of the brunch, assemble the chicken rolls. Remove sauce and filling from the refrigerator to bring to room temperature. Flatten the chicken thighs between sheets of dampened greaseproof paper or cling film. Trim the sides to neaten if necessary. Sprinkle with salt and pepper and spread with about a tablespoon of spinach filling. Roll up, beginning with a short side. Tie in two places with white cotton thread to hold shape.

7. Melt butter in a large skillet. Fry chicken rolls over medium heat, turning often until browned on all sides – about 10 minutes. Remove from heat – cut and discard threads.

8. Spoon the tomato carrot sauce into a baking dish large enough to hold the chicken rolls in one layer. Place the chicken rolls in the dish. Heat the oven to 180C/350F/gas 4. About 15 minutes before serving, cover the dish with aluminium foil and bake, until warmed through.

SULTANA ROSEMARY BUNS

This flavour combination is one I remember from purchasing Italian bread at Convito Italiano in Wilmette, Illinois.

MAKES 12
15g/½oz sachet dried yeast
1 teaspoon honey
250g/8oz plain flour
175g/6oz 100% wholemeal flour
2 tablespoons wheat germ
1 teaspoon salt
½ teaspoon dried rosemary, crushed
75g/3oz sultanas
oil for greasing
a little semolina for sprinkling
TO GLAZE
1 large egg yolk
¼ teaspoon salt

1. Sprinkle yeast over 225ml/8fl. oz lukewarm water. Stir in honey, and let stand until spongy.

2. Add flours, wheat germ, salt, rosemary and sultanas, stirring to make a soft dough. Knead for 5 to 8 minutes, adding more plain flour as necessary.

3. Place in an oiled bowl, turning to oil dough evenly. Cover with a cloth and let rise in a warm place until doubled in size.

4. Punch dough down. Turn out on to a board and let rest for a few minutes. Divide dough into 12 balls and flatten them slightly.

5. Place balls on a tray which has been oiled and sprinkled with semolina. With a sharp knife, cut a slit across the top of each bun. Beat together egg yolk, 1 teaspoon water and salt, use to brush tops and sides of buns. Cover lightly with a cloth and leave to rise for 20-30 minutes.

6. Heat oven to 200C/400F/gas 6 and bake buns for 20-25 minutes until golden brown.

Facing page: crudités (top); sultana rosemary buns (bottom). Above: fruit salad vinaigrette

---

FRUIT SALAD VINAIGRETTE

This crisp fruit and vegetable salad has a spicy dressing which adds a refreshingly piquant note to the meal.

SERVES 6

lettuce, chicory and endive, as available
1 mango, cut in wedges and peeled
1 ogen or galia melon, halved, seeded and made into melon balls or chunks
1 tart green apple, cored and sliced
FOR THE DRESSING
½ teaspoon anchovy paste
½ teaspoon grated lemon zest
½ teaspoon sugar
2 tablespoons freshly squeezed lemon juice
2 tablespoons white wine vinegar
1 teaspoon finely chopped fresh dill
freshly ground pepper
4-6 tablespoons walnut oil

1. Combine dressing ingredients in a jar with a tight-fitting lid. Seal jar and shake well. Set aside to let the flavours blend.

2. Arrange salad vegetables and fruit on a flat plate; just before serving, shake dressing again and drizzle over top.

WINE NOTES

Brunchable champagne need not be costly grande marque. *Some of the supermarkets have the ability and purchasing clout to find good champagne at bargain prices. The difficulty on more formal occasions is that there is no certain consistency about their style, but at an informal buffet brunch guests will not complain. If you prefer to offer cocktails, you can economize further and use cheaper sparkling wine—such as* vin mousseux *by G. F. Cavalier, Crémant d'Alsace or Crémant de Bourgogne.*

Brunch wine should clearly come from America: there are very classy California Chardonnays to be had from producers such as Clos de Bois, Edna Valley, Hawk Crest and Stratford Vineyards—but do not serve them too heavily chilled.

Ann Long

WINTER DINNER PARTY

In the deep midwinter, Ann Long's elegant menu brightens a long, dark evening

---

Chicken-liver mousses with peppered centres

Loin of venison in puff-pastry parcels with plum sauce
Broccoli florets
Parsnip purée

Medley of fruits in a rich almond cream, with orange rum sauce

---

Many of our friends and guests have never seen me without an apron. I spend almost every minute of every working day in the kitchen, because I cook for a living. I enjoy my work, and feel a keen sense of pleasure in seeing my sweet or savoury sauces develop a lovely, clear sheen, or in unmoulding a mousse that looks and smells appetizing and perhaps hides a surprise flavour in its centre.

My enjoyment in presenting my guests with an element of surprise leads me to conceal tasty stuffings in savoury foods, and to contrast colours and flavours in sauces and garnishes, so that the results appeal to the eye as well as to the palate.

Everything must be fresh and must look fresh, too. To achieve this effect with vegetables, I cook them quickly in plenty of lightly salted boiling water. To do this, cook them in a wire spaghetti-basket so that draining them is no problem.

Presenting a dish attractively calls for a pleasing arrangement of food and a garnish for savoury dishes, and for some decoration of sweet dishes, but this must not be excessive. If you decide to use piped cream to decorate a cake but are nervous about spoiling its appearance, pipe the cream on to the plate surrounding it; a mistake is easy to wipe off a plate. A very simple but effective idea is to place a vividly coloured flower on or beside a cake or pudding to enhance its appearance.

For me, trying a new recipe is always exciting, and devising variations brings fresh charm to well-loved favourites. I always read any recipe right through to make sure I have all the equipment and ingredients.

Of course, creative cooking is an art; it requires effort and entails a measure of stress, even stage-fright, as the time for serving your creations approaches. To help me stay calm, I have developed the habit of making lists of ingredients and equipment I shall need and of tasks to be done at each stage of preparation. I find that seeing each item safely crossed off gives me a much-needed surge of confidence.

If your preparation has been planned in stages and carefully checked against the lists, it will not seem too daunting, nor too laborious, because at each stage you will be able to see that nothing has been forgotten. With this support to your peace of mind you, the host or hostess, who are also the chef, should have time on the day of the dinner to attend to your own appearance and to enjoy the party.

Whether you are a professional chef or are entertaining at home, the whole point of creative cooking is that it should lead to a pleasurable, satisfying experience shared by the person who gives, and those who attend, the party.

CHICKEN-LIVER MOUSSES WITH PEPPERED CENTRES

SERVES 6

hazelnut oil
350g/12oz chicken livers
(untrimmed weight)
25g/1oz butter
1 tablespoon lemon juice
150ml/¼pt home-made mayonnaise
¼ teaspoon ground coriander
freshly ground black pepper
1 tablespoon aspic powder, dissolved in
150ml/¼pt boiling water
300ml/½pt double cream
1 egg white
salad leaves to garnish
toast to serve
FOR THE PEPPERED CENTRES
1 teaspoon green peppercorns
½ teaspoon pink peppercorns
4 tablespoons freshly chopped parsley

1. Using a pastry brush, paint the insides of 6 coffee cups or 150ml/¼pt ramekins with hazelnut oil.

Mix together the peppercorns and parsley for the centre.

2. With a sharp stainless-steel knife, trim away and discard the white, stringy tissue and any flesh tinged with green from the livers. Cut each liver into eighths; put the pieces in a bowl large enough to hold them in a single layer. Pour over boiling water to cover and leave them for 5 minutes to firm up the texture of the livers. Using a slotted spoon, lay them on absorbent paper to dry.

3. Heat the butter with a little hazelnut oil in a frying pan. Sauté the livers over a medium heat, turning them often, for about 3 minutes, until they lose their pinkness. Using a slotted spoon, transfer the livers on to a plate lined with absorbent paper and leave them to cool.

4. Place the cooled livers in a food processor; blend to a smooth paste with the lemon juice and mayonnaise. Add the seasonings. Pour 4 tablespoons of liquid aspic into the livers and blend again until completely smooth.

5. Pour the double cream into a bowl; whisk until the cream holds its shape. Sieve the liver purée on to the whipped

COUNTDOWN

Two or three days before
• *Make the orange rum sauce.*
• *Marinate the venison.*

Two days before
• *Soak the dried fruit and nuts with the spiced rum.*

The day before
• *Prepare the puff pastry; if you use frozen, leave it to defrost in the refrigerator overnight.*
• *Soak the chicken livers in milk if liked (see Note).*
• *Make the almond cream dessert; plum sauce; parsnip purée.*

In the morning
• *Make the chicken-liver mousses and chill them.*
• *Prepare the venison parcels and leave in the refrigerator.*

Two hours before
• *Unwrap the dessert and return it to the refrigerator.*

Just before serving
• *Set the oven to 220C/425F/ gas 7.*
• *Heat the baking tray.*
• *Turn out the chicken-liver mousses; garnish and make the toast.*

During the first course
• *Cook the venison parcels and broccoli.*
• *Reheat the plum sauce and parsnip purée.*

cream then, using a metal spoon, gently fold them together. In another bowl whisk the egg white to the soft-peak stage; fold into the mousse. Adjust the seasoning if necessary. Half-fill the prepared moulds with the mousse mixture and chill them for 5-10 minutes, until the surface of each mousse is just firm to the touch.

6. Using a teaspoon, place a little of the peppered filling on the centre of each set layer and then cover with the rest of the mousse. Cover the mousses with cling film and return to the refrigerator to set.

7. To serve, run a thin knife around each mousse; turn out on to individual plates. Garnish with salad leaves and serve with toast.

Note:

For delicately coloured mousses, soak the chicken livers overnight first in a little milk.

LOIN OF VENISON IN PUFF-PASTRY PARCELS WITH PLUM SAUCE

When ordering venison you may have to buy a whole saddle. For this recipe you need 6 boned and well-trimmed eye of loin pieces weighing 150g/5oz each. I suggest that the rest of the saddle should be trimmed, portioned and individually wrapped in cling film, then frozen. You can also freeze the trimmings totally covered in the wine marinade, and use them later to make delicious burgers or pâté.

SERVES 6

6 × 150g/5oz trimmed loin pieces of venison, or boned loin chops
oil to seal the venison
175g/6oz carrots
175g/6oz courgettes
butter for sautéeing
350g/12oz made-weight puff pastry
tarragon leaves
freshly ground black pepper
flour for dusting
beaten egg for glazing

FOR THE MARINADE
1 unpeeled onion, thinly sliced
1 garlic clove, sliced
1 orange, quartered
1 teaspoon dried thyme
$\frac{1}{4}$ nutmeg, grated
3 black peppercorns
300ml/$\frac{1}{2}$pt red wine
1 tablespoon sunflower oil
150ml/$\frac{1}{4}$pt chicken stock
FOR THE PLUM SAUCE
500g/1lb stoned plums or 570g/18oz can plums, well drained and stoned
150ml/$\frac{1}{4}$pt red wine
3 tablespoons redcurrant jelly
$\frac{1}{2}$ teaspoon cinnamon
grated nutmeg
1 tablespoon coarse-grain mustard
1 tablespoon orange juice

1. Using a sharp knife, cut away all the tough membrane from the surface of each piece of meat. Place the venison pieces side by side in a non-metallic dish. Place all the dry marinade ingredients around the meat and pour over the wine, oil and chicken stock. Then cover the open dish and leave it in a cool place for 2 to 3 days, turning occasionally, to allow the flavours to mingle.

2. To make the plum sauce, cook the plums in the wine until tender, add the redcurrant jelly and stir it with a wooden spoon until the jelly has dissolved. Ladle the cooked fruit and juice into a blender and lightly purée. Blend in the remaining sauce ingredients and chill until needed.

3. Take the meat out of the dish and dry the pieces thoroughly with a cloth. In a frying pan heat enough oil to cover the base and lightly seal the venison pieces 3 at a time. Lay the meat on a tray covered with absorbent paper and chill.

4. Using a thin, sharp knife, cut the carrots and courgettes lengthways into thin slices and trim each strip to the same length as the venison pieces. Melt enough butter to coat the bottom of the frying pan; sauté the vegetables a few strips at a time in a single layer, turning them once. When they are coloured, remove them with a spatula and drain them on absorbent paper.

5. Roll out the pastry very thinly to form a large square. Take the venison pieces out of the fridge and arrange the vegetable strips on top of each one, sprinkle with tarragon leaves and season with black pepper.

6. Cut the pastry into 6 rectangles 10 × 23cm/4 × 9in. Place a piece of venison, vegetable-side up, at one narrow end of each pastry rectangle, brush water round the edges and fold the pastry over the meat. Press the borders together and trim the edges. Use your fingertips to press and imprint the cut edge to form a pattern and to seal firmly.

7. Cut 6 hearts out of the pastry scraps, dampen with water and press one on to the side of each parcel. Make an air hole in the top of each parcel. Place them on a lightly floured tray and chill for at least 30 minutes.

8. Heat the oven to 220C/425F/gas 7 and heat a large baking tray in the top half of the oven. Brush the parcels with egg glaze and cook them on the baking tray near the top of the oven until golden and crisp; 15 minutes for rose-coloured meat. Serve the parcels on the heated plum sauce, accompanied by parsnip purée (see following recipe) and crisply cooked broccoli florets.

PARSNIP PURÉE

SERVES 6

| 100g/4oz butter |
| 250g/8oz onions, chopped |
| 1kg/2lb parsnips, cut into chunks |
| 300ml/½pt sherry or chicken stock |
| salt and pepper |
| 150ml/¼pt double cream (optional) |

1. Melt the butter in a saucepan and gently cook the onions; add the parsnips and stir well. Pour in the sherry or stock. Cover the pan with a sheet of greaseproof paper and the saucepan lid. Turn down the heat as low as possible and cook for about 30 minutes until very tender. Liquidize to a purée and sieve.

2. Taste, then season. Stir in double cream if you prefer a thinner purée. Taste again for seasoning. Leave to cool; you can keep this covered in the refrigerator for up to 2 to 3 days. Gently reheat the purée before serving.

MEDLEY OF FRUITS IN A RICH ALMOND CREAM, WITH ORANGE RUM SAUCE

SERVES 6

| 175-250g/6-8oz dried fruit and nuts (e.g. figs, prunes, apricots and pistachio nuts) |
| 125ml/4fl. oz rum |
| 1 clove |
| 4 allspice berries |
| 2 oranges |
| 1 teaspoon sugar |
| 175ml/6fl. oz double cream |
| 2 egg yolks |
| about 100g/4oz caster sugar |
| 275g/10oz cream cheese |
| 175g/6oz unsalted butter, melted and cooled |
| 1 teaspoon Amaretto liqueur |
| 100g/4oz ground almonds |

1. Tip the fruit and nuts into a small bowl and stir in the rum and spices. Leave for 2 days to soak, turning the fruit occasionally.

2. Using a hot, long needle, pierce 5 holes in the base of an oblong plastic box (24 × 15cm/10 × 6in and 6cm/2½in deep) to make a draining dish. Rinse a clean tea towel in cold water, wring it out and drape it over the prepared dish so that it overlaps the edges.

3. Arrange the marinated fruit and nuts on a tray lined with absorbent paper and reserve the spiced rum.

4. Peel the rind off each orange, and cut into long matchsticks. Place the rind in a saucepan with 1 teaspoon sugar, 225ml/8fl. oz cold water and 2 tablespoons of the spiced rum (reserving the rest for the orange rum sauce), bring to the boil, then gently simmer for 1 minute.

5. Pour the liquid and cooked rind into a sieve set over a bowl and leave to drain, then dry the strips on absorbent paper.

6. To make the custard, pour the cream into a saucepan and set it over a low heat to boil. In a bowl, blend the egg yolks with 25g/1oz caster sugar, using a wooden spoon. Boil the cream for 2 minutes, then pour it on to the beaten egg mixture; stir until smooth, then set the bowl over a pan of gently simmering water, stirring until little bubbles appear around the edges. Remove the bowl from the heat. Stir the custard until it cools, then ladle it into a jug.

7. Beat the cream cheese with the remaining caster sugar to a smooth, creamy consistency. Gradually pour in the melted butter and stir until the mixture is smooth and creamy. Stir in the Amaretto and ground almonds.

8. Gradually stir the cooled custard into the almond cream. Using a sharp knife, cut the marinated fruits lengthways into strips. Cover the base of the draining dish with a smooth layer of almond cream and carefully arrange the fruit in rows along the length of the cream. Continue filling the mould with alternate layers of cream, nuts and fruit, finishing with a smooth, thin layer of cream. Cover with a layer of the prepared orange rind. Fold the loose ends of the tea towel over the top; rest the dish on a tray to catch the drips and chill overnight.

9. To serve, unwrap the loose ends of the tea towel, place a plate over the dish and invert them both. Lift off the dish and carefully peel away the material. Slice the almond cream at the table with a serrated knife. Pour some orange rum sauce (see following recipe) on to each plate.

ORANGE RUM SAUCE

SERVES 6

| 500g/1lb caster sugar |
| 300ml/½pt hot water, mixed with the juice and finely grated zest of 1 orange and 1 lemon |
| 1 lemon, scrubbed |
| 2 tablespoons spiced rum (reserved from almond cream recipe) |

WINE NOTES

The essential point to remember here is that the bright fruit sauces will require ample and complementary fruit flavour from the wine if they are to hold their own.

Happily there are always some scrumptiously fruity wines about from producers of the modern school, even in such classic and sometimes austere areas as Burgundy, Bordeaux and Rioja. The ripe and sweet raspberry tang of well-made Bourgogne Pinot Noir will go deliciously with the chicken liver mousse, or for those who must economize, a light, direct and uncomplicated Rioja can show an attractive bite of raspberry fruit as well.

For the venison, I would like a weightier, but still lively, wine—from the Rhône or Italy most probably. There are some superb Italian Dolcettos to be had, with brilliant colour and cherry-plum flavours, while some of the best Côtes-du-Rhônes can be as lavishly plummy and spicy as first-class Châteauneuf-du-Pape.

For the fruit and almond cream, an exceptional Italian dessert wine that would depart from the conventional routine of Sauternes or tawny port is Vino Liquoroso Torcolato of Maculan. It costs a bit, though.

1. Pour the caster sugar into a saucepan and shake the pan so that the sugar settles evenly. Pour in 600ml/1pt cold water and bring slowly to the boil without stirring. Turn up the heat; let the syrup bubble until it turns pale gold, then amber.

2. Off the heat, carefully pour in the hot citrus water and return the pan to a low heat. Stir the syrup with a wooden spoon until it is smooth and boiling gently.

3. Place the whole lemon in a container that has a lid; pour the syrup over and stir in the rum.

4. When the sauce is cold, seal with the lid and leave for a few days to allow the flavours to mingle.

Caroline Waldegrave

CHRISTMAS DINNER

Caroline Waldegrave has updated this most traditional of meals with a carefully planned menu featuring both old and new

Marinated salmon and melon salad

Roast goose Marie-Claire with cranberry and orange sauce
Broccoli and cauliflower with sesame seeds
Roast potatoes
Crunchy salad

Vanilla bombe with prunes

COUNTDOWN

Two weeks before
• *Make the bombe.*

On Christmas Eve
• *Prepare and marinate the salmon.*
• *Make the goose stock.*
• *Prepare the stuffing.*
• *Make the cranberry sauce, if wished.*
• *Wash and dry the salad leaves and put in the refrigerator to crisp.*

Four hours before the meal
• *Heat the oven to 190C/375F/ gas 5 and stuff the goose.*
• *Put the goose in the oven (assuming that it weighs about 5kg/11lb and needs 3 hours and 10 minutes' cooking time and ½ hour resting time).*

While the goose is cooking
• *Prepare the salmon and melon salad and arrange on 6 plates; cover each with cling film and put in the refrigerator.*
• *Make the cranberry sauce, if not done.*
• *Parboil the potatoes.*
• *After the goose has been cooking for 1 hour, drain off the fat; add fat to the potatoes and put them in to roast.*

Forty minutes before dinner
• *Baste the goose with honey.*
• *Put the plates and serving dishes to warm.*
• *Make the French dressing, prepare and dress the crunchy salad.*
• *Transfer the cooked goose to a serving dish and leave in the oven.* ▶

I am, I suppose, what is called a health food enthusiast; our diet at home is low in fat, low in salt and high in fresh fruit and vegetables. But Christmas provides the perfect excuse to relax the rules.

Not that I enjoy overeating – there is no fun in feeling so bloated that when you sit down to listen to the Queen you doubt whether you will ever be able to stand up again.

For Christmas I try to prepare a meal which has a good balance of both indulgent and healthy food. Salad and fresh fruit rub shoulders with roast goose and a luxurious ice cream bombe. Guests can choose to be wicked or worthy, or both!

The salmon and melon starter is simple and refreshing to whet the appetite for the rich main course which follows. I have chosen goose as I think turkey is the dullest of meats, and the tradition of having a goose actually goes much further

back than does the fashion for turkey. Brussels sprouts are abandoned in favour of broccoli and cauliflower served with sesame seeds, but I have stuck to roast potatoes as they are truly delicious. And as I never think of a meal as complete without a salad, there is a crunchy salad accompaniment, too.

I adore Christmas pudding but find it too heavy after a full-blown festive lunch, so as an alternative dessert I would serve a bombe – it's just as wickedly calorific, but it gives a lighter touch to the end of the meal. When serving the bombe I would also put out a huge bowl of satsumas and another of unshelled walnuts and brazil nuts.

If you're playing host, the secret of enjoying yourself in this situation is to plan ahead as much as you can, so that when the big day dawns, you can afford to relax. I hope to buy all my presents, cards, crackers and

extra drink several weeks ahead. By the middle of December, I'll have ordered the goose and the tree, and frozen the bombe. In the week of Christmas, I'll do all the last minute shopping, not forgetting extra supplies of essentials such as coffee and loo paper. Christmas Eve will, I hope, see me decorating the tree, putting up the decorations – no doubt hiding the dirty washing and making sure I know *exactly* where the corkscrew is!

MARINATED SALMON AND MELON SALAD

A light and refreshing first course, which has a classic dressing made luxurious with subtle hazelnut oil.

SERVES 6

350g/12oz piece fresh salmon fillet
juice of 2 limes
18 green peppercorns, rinsed if in brine, plus 3-4 to garnish
2 handfuls bitter salad leaves – watercress, chicory, baby spinach or endive
1 small melon
FOR THE DRESSING
5 tablespoons hazelnut oil
1 tablespoon white wine vinegar
salt and freshly ground pepper

1. Slice the salmon finely and marinate in a cool place in the lime juice and green peppercorns for a minimum of 24 hours, and a maximum of 36 hours. Turn occasionally.
2. Wash and shake dry the salad leaves, and put them in the refrigerator in a polythene bag overnight.
3. Cut the melon in half and scoop out the seeds. Quarter the melon, remove the skin and slice the flesh finely.
4. Mix together the oil and vinegar for the dressing, then season to taste.
5. To serve, arrange the salad leaves on 6 small plates and place slices of salmon and melon on top. Drizzle over the dressing and garnish with a few green peppercorns.

ROAST GOOSE MARIE-CLAIRE WITH CRANBERRY AND ORANGE SAUCE

This may seem a huge bird for just six people, but most of a goose seems to be carcass. Here the bird is stuffed with a delicious slightly Middle Eastern mixture.

SERVES 6

4.5-5kg/10-11lb goose, with giblets
salt and freshly ground pepper
½ lemon
1 tablespoon honey
bunch of watercress to garnish
FOR THE GRAVY
goose giblets
1 onion, sliced
1 bay leaf
5 black peppercorns
stalk of fresh parsley
2 tablespoons calvados
FOR THE STUFFING
25g/1oz butter
1 onion, finely chopped
275g/10oz chicken breast, minced or cut in 4 if using a food processor
1 tablespoon roughly chopped fresh sage
350g/12oz dessert apples, peeled and chopped
10 dried apricots, soaked for 2 hours, then drained and chopped
50g/2oz shredded beef suet
75g/3oz fresh breadcrumbs
1 size 3 egg
50g/2oz unsalted pistachio nuts, roughly chopped
FOR THE CRANBERRY SAUCE
700g/1½lb fresh or frozen cranberries
250g/8oz sugar
50ml/2fl. oz orange juice

1. Make the goose stock for the gravy a day in advance. Remove the giblets from the bird, rinse and put in a pan with the onion, bay leaf, peppercorns, parsley stalk and 850ml/1½pt water. Simmer for about an hour. Remove from the heat and strain. Keep refrigerated until needed.

Countdown (continued)

Just before serving
• *Cook the cauliflower and broccoli and place in a heated serving dish. Do not add the sesame seeds yet.*
• *Transfer the roast potatoes to a heated serving dish.*
• *Remove the cling film from the salmon and melon salad and drizzle over the French dressing.*

After the first course
• *Remove the bombe from the freezer ready to turn out.*
• *Sprinkle sesame seeds over the cauliflower and broccoli and serve immediately.*

2. While the goose stock is simmering, make the cranberry sauce. Put the sauce ingredients and 150ml/¼pt water into a heavy saucepan. Bring to the boil and simmer slowly, stirring occasionally, for 30 minutes, until the sauce looks like liquid jam. Set aside.

3. The stuffing can also be prepared the day ahead. Melt the butter, add the onion and cook for about 10 minutes until soft but not coloured. In a food processor, beat together the chicken breast, onion, sage, apples, apricots and suet. Add enough of the breadcrumbs to make a firm but not solid stuffing.

Season to taste. Add the egg and beat it in thoroughly. Stir in the pistachio nuts. Cool.

4. Wipe the goose all over outside and remove any feather stubble. Remove the lumps of fat inside the body cavity. Rinse very well inside. Season the inside with salt and pepper, then rub with a cut lemon.

5. Heat the oven to 190C/375F/gas 5. Pierce the bird all over with a needle or fork, then stuff. Weigh goose to establish cooking time (allow 35 minutes per kg/15 minutes per lb plus an extra 15 minutes). Sprinkle with salt. Place on a

wire rack in a roasting tin. Cook for calculated time, basting occasionally, but do not worry if you forget as goose is a fatty bird. Remove the fat from the roasting tin every so often with a plastic baster and reserve it for roasting the potatoes. If the goose starts to get too dark, cover it with foil. Be careful not to overcook the goose or it will become tough and dry.

6. Ten minutes before the bird is done, spread the honey evenly over the skin. This will help to make it crisp. Once the goose is cooked, transfer it to a serving plate, remove wing tips and thread, and

return to the oven, now turned off.

7. Make the gravy. Carefully spoon off any remaining fat from the roasting tin and pour the remaining cooking juices into a saucepan. Add the goose stock and a little of the stuffing scooped out from the goose. Bring to the boil, whisk well and simmer for about 15 minutes. (If you are serving the cranberry sauce hot, reheat it in a small saucepan while the gravy is simmering.) Increase the heat and boil the gravy until syrupy, then add the calvados, season to taste and boil for 30 seconds. Strain into a warmed gravy boat.

8. To serve, sit the goose on a bed of watercress and serve gravy and cranberry sauce separately.

Note:

It is very important to remove all the fat from the goose vent. If left in, it will melt into the stuffing and make it inedible.

BROCCOLI AND CAULIFLOWER WITH SESAME SEEDS

The crisp, crunchy texture of sesame seeds complements goose very well.

SERVES 6

1 small cauliflower
500g/1lb broccoli
1 heaped tablespoon sesame seeds

1. Break the cauliflower and broccoli into florets, and cook in boiling salted water until just tender, about 5 minutes.
2. While the vegetables are cooking, dry fry the sesame seeds in a saucepan over a moderate heat. When they begin to pop, cover with a lid to prevent them jumping out, and shake for 30 seconds.
3. Drain the cauliflower and broccoli and transfer to a warmed serving dish. Sprinkle with the seeds before serving.

ROAST POTATOES

SERVES 6

1.4kg/3lb potatoes
goose fat
salt and pepper

1. Wash and peel the potatoes. Put them into a saucepan of salted water, bring to the boil and cook for 5 minutes.
2. Drain cooked potatoes using a sieve and toss gently so that they begin to look crumbly.
3. Take some of the hot goose fat from the roasting tin and put it into a second roasting tin. Tip in the potatoes, turn well, season and roast for 1-1½ hours, turning once to colour them.

CRUNCHY SALAD

SERVES 6

2 dessert apples
1 head celery
50g/2oz walnuts
French dressing (for recipe, see marinated salmon and melon salad)

1. Core and chop the apples.
2. Wash the celery and separate into stalks, tearing off any stringy parts. Chop into bite-sized pieces.
3. Roughly chop the walnuts.
4. Mix everything together, then toss in a little French dressing.

VANILLA BOMBE WITH PRUNES

Made in the shape of a Christmas pudding, this bombe is filled with dried prunes and masses of port.

SERVES 6

150g/5oz caster sugar
1 vanilla pod or 1 teaspoon vanilla essence
6 large egg yolks
850ml/1½pt double cream, lightly whipped
FOR THE FILLING
350g/12oz dried, stoned prunes, soaked overnight in 600ml/1pt cold tea and drained
100g/4oz granulated sugar
150ml/¼pt port

1. First, make the ice cream. Put the sugar, vanilla pod or essence and 200ml/7fl. oz of water into a saucepan and dissolve over a gentle heat, stirring occasionally. When the sugar is dissolved, bring to the boil and boil until a teaspoon of the hot syrup forms threads between two teaspoons when they are drawn apart (90C/200F on a sugar thermometer). Allow the syrup to cool for 1 minute. Remove vanilla pod, if using, before continuing.
2. Whisk the egg yolks and pour on the syrup while whisking. Beat until the

WINE NOTES

mixture is thick and mousse-like.

3. Set aside to cool, whisking occasionally.

4. Fold in the whipped cream, pour into the freezer container and freeze. When the ice cream is half frozen, whisk again then return to the freezer to set.

5. Place a 1.5L/2½pt pudding basin in the freezer while you soften the ice cream slightly at room temperature. Pack two-thirds of the vanilla ice cream evenly around the base and sides of the basin, smoothing the inside with a spoon. Return to the freezer with the rest of the ice cream.

6. Meanwhile, put the prunes and sugar in a saucepan, cover with water and cook gently for about 20 minutes, so that the prunes do not break up. Pour in the port and leave the mixture to cool completely.

7. Remove the ice cream for the top of the bombe from the freezer, to soften slightly.

8. Pour prunes and port into the centre of the ice cream. Cover with the remaining ice cream, place cling film over the top and freeze again.

9. To turn out, take the bombe out of the freezer 20 minutes before you want to unmould it. Put a serving plate on top of the basin, turn the basin and plate over together, shake well and lift off the basin. If it is still a little reluctant, stick a knife right through the centre of the bombe to the base of the bowl. This will release the vacuum, making it easier to turn out.

Note:

When packing the ice cream into the basin, if it begins to melt, just return it to the freezer for a while to make it more manageable.

Shehzad Husain

INDIAN VEGETARIAN DINNER

Non-meat eaters are often neglected at Christmas – for them Shehzad Husain's dinner provides an exciting alternative to traditional dishes

Chewra – *Split peas with flaked rice, cashews and raisins*

Masalay dar aloo – *Spicy potato curry*
Matar pulao – *Aromatic pea pulao*
Bhindi – *Okra*
Dhaal – *Gingered red lentils*
Crunchy mooli salad

Kheer – *Indian rice pudding*

As Christmas approaches, I start thinking of the growing number of vegetarians who, I am sure, feel alienated from the rest of the population and the seasonal surroundings. Almost everywhere you look you see turkeys, huge chickens or enormous joints which must be disconcerting to the non-meat eaters among us.

Traditionally, and for religious reasons, the majority of Indians are vegetarians and consider their meat-eating compatriots as the exception rather than the norm — so much so that that they label them 'non-vegetarians'! Over the years, consequently, an abundance of vegetarian delicacies has evolved and been perfected in the sub-Continent. These dishes are rich in variety and a healthy substitute for meat — and are by no means restricted to vegetarians only. I suggest that all those who enjoy Indian food should try vegetarian cooking as well.

The majority of our vegetarian menus include lentils or pulses of some sort, as these are rich in protein. There are many different types to choose from. Dhaal, or lentils, are probably among the most commonly used in the Indian kitchen and are easy to cook. My vegetarian Christmas dinner also includes curried okra — simple to cook and a delicious introduction to this very unusual and tasty vegetable; and, as a healthy and tasty alternative to the usual crisps or peanuts with cocktails, the *chewra*, which is sure to impress your guests.

Another favourite of mine is *masalay dar aaloo*, or spicy potatoes, an additional, fairly dry, curry with an unusually pleasant spicy flavour. To complement the okra curry and *masalay dar aaloo*, I have included *matar pulao*, a delightful and colourful rice dish which is always a favourite of Indian food epicures.

To round off the meal, I have chosen a traditional rice pudding, *Kheer*, garnished with silver leaf for a festive effect. I hope you enjoy preparing these very simple — but extremely delicious — dishes, and wish you every success.

COUNTDOWN

The day before
• *Make the chewra and store in an airtight tin.*
• *Soak the chick peas for the crunchy mooli salad.*

In the morning
• *Make the kheer, cover and refrigerate.*
• *Cook the dhaal, cover and chill.*
• *Cook the chick peas.*

About one hour before the meal
• *Prepare the vegetables for the salad, add the chick peas, lemon juice and salt. Cover and chill.*
• *Wash and dry the lettuce leaves; put in bags to crisp in the refrigerator.*
• *Prepare garnishes for the pulao.*

About 45 minutes before the meal
• *Cook the spicy potatoes, and keep warm in a low oven.*

About 20 minutes before the meal
• *Cook the okra.*

About 10 minutes before serving
• *Chop the coriander for the garnishes.*

5 minutes before serving
• *Arrange the lettuce and vegetables for the salad on serving platter and garnish.*
• *Prepare a double boiler and reheat kheer, if serving warm.*
• *Reheat the dhaal.*

Just before serving
• *Transfer the chewra to a dish, serve with aperitifs.*

After the first course
• *Make the baghaars for the potatoes and dhaal, pour over each dish and garnish.*

CHEWRA
Split peas with flaked rice, cashews and raisins

Mixes like this are served any time of the day, with drinks or tea. You can make a large quantity and store in an airtight container as a change from crisps.

If you have difficulty obtaining curry leaves, omit them.

SERVES 6

50g/2oz chana dhaal or split yellow peas
300ml/½pt corn oil
½ teaspoon onion seeds (kalongi)
6 curry leaves
250g/8oz flaked rice (pawa)
25g/1oz cashew nuts
25g/1oz raisins
75g/3oz sugar
1 teaspoon salt
1 teaspoon chilli powder

1. Wash the *chana dhaal*, then soak for at least 3 hours. Heat the oil in a saucepan and fry the onion seeds and curry leaves. Add the flaked rice and fry until crisp and golden (making sure the mixture does not burn). Using a slotted spoon, remove the mixture from the pan and place on a small tray lined with kitchen paper to absorb any excess oil.
2. Tip the mixture into a bowl. Fry the cashew nuts in the remaining oil, remove with a slotted spoon, and mix with the flaked rice. Then add the raisins, sugar, salt and chilli powder and mix everything together.
3. Reheat the oil remaining in the saucepan and fry the drained *chana dhaal* until golden brown. Drain on kitchen paper, then add to the bowl and mix everything together. It can be served immediately or stored in an airtight tin.

Note:
Flaked rice, or *pawa*, is available from Indian grocers and larger supermarkets.

MASALAY DAR ALOO
Spicy potato curry

This is a delicious, semi-dry potato curry which has a very spicy, tangy flavour. When new potatoes are in season I prefer to use them whole, as they do improve the appearance and flavour. However, ordinary potatoes cut into cubes are almost as good. Serve these with a *baghaar* dressing.

The whole dried red chillies used for the baghaar can be quite fiery if you accidentally bite on them. So either warn your guests to discard them, or omit them from the *baghaar* to be on the safe side. This will not alter the flavour, it will only reduce the heat.

SERVES 6

6 tablespoons corn oil
500g/1lb onions, peeled and finely chopped
1 teaspoon puréed fresh ginger
1 teaspoon puréed fresh garlic
1 teaspoon chilli powder
1 teaspoon ground cumin
1 teaspoon ground coriander
1 teaspoon salt
2 tablespoons tomato purée
500g/1lb new potatoes, scrubbed, or old potatoes, peeled and cut into 4cm/1½in cubes
75g/3oz green pepper, sliced
FOR THE *BAGHAAR*
½ teaspoon onion seeds (kalongi)
½ teaspoon yellow mustard seeds
½ teaspoon fenugreek seeds
3 whole dried red chillies, seeded (optional)
1 chopped green chilli and 1 tablespoon chopped fresh coriander to garnish

1. Heat the oil in a large pan and fry the onions until golden brown. Add the ginger and garlic and cook for a further 2-3 minutes.
2. Mix together all the other spices and salt with the tomato purée. Lower the heat and add the spice and tomato purée to the onions; stir-fry with a wooden spoon for 1-2 minutes, scraping the bottom of the pan. Then add the potatoes and stir well.
3. Add the sliced pepper and 200ml/7fl oz water, cover the pan, and simmer over a low heat for 20-30 minutes or until the potatoes are tender. Transfer to a bowl.
4. To make the *baghaar*, heat the oil in a pan and throw in the seeds and dried red chillies, if using. Fry all these until they turn a shade darker. Turn off the heat. Pour this sizzling dressing over the top of the spicy potatoes.
5. Just before serving, garnish with chopped green chillies and chopped coriander.

MATAR PULAO
Aromatic pea pulao

This rice dish is certainly one of my favourites, and it makes a colourful centrepiece for any special occasion meal.

It is always advisable to use whole spices for rice dishes, because they add subtle flavouring and a beautiful aroma to the rice. Though the whole spices are edible, it is best not to eat them as they have a rather sharp flavour which may spoil the taste of the dish; it is quite acceptable to leave any whole spices on the side of the plate. Always use a steel slotted spoon to handle the rice. For Indian rice dishes I would recommend using basmati rice.

SERVES 6

700g/1½lb basmati rice
100g/4oz unsalted butter
1 tablespoon corn oil
100g/4oz onions, sliced
1 teaspoon black cumin seeds
4 whole black peppercorns
3 whole cloves
4 whole green cardamoms
2 tablespoons freshly chopped coriander
1 green chilli, chopped
2 teaspoons salt
175g/6oz frozen peas
2 firm tomatoes thinly sliced, and 2 hard-boiled eggs thinly sliced, to garnish

1. Wash the rice three times, running your fingers through and gently rubbing the grains.
2. Heat the butter in a heavy-based saucepan with the oil; add the sliced onion and fry until golden brown. Add the black cumin seeds, black peppercorns, cloves and cardamoms, lower the heat and stir-fry for a further minute. Add half the fresh coriander, the chilli and the rice. Stir-fry the mixture for 2 more minutes, adding the salt. While stirring, scrape the bottom of the pan to prevent the rice from sticking.
3. Pour in 850ml/1½pt water and bring to the boil. Lower the heat and stir in the peas. Cover the saucepan with a tight-fitting lid and cook for about 20 minutes or until the moisture has been absorbed.
4. Check to see if the rice is cooked right through, then, using a slotted spoon, gently transfer the rice and peas to an oval-shaped serving dish.
5. Garnish with thinly sliced tomatoes and sliced eggs. Sprinkle over the remaining fresh coriander. Serve hot.

BHINDI
Okra

SERVES 6

5 tablespoons corn oil
350g/12oz onions, sliced
500g/1lb okra
175g/6oz red pepper, seeded and sliced
1 teaspoon salt
1 teaspoon puréed fresh ginger
1 or 2 green chillies (seeded if desired)
2 tablespoons freshly chopped coriander to garnish

1. Heat the oil in a large frying pan. Fry the onions until golden brown. Cut the okra into 2.5cm/1in slices and add them to the pan with the red pepper.
2. Add the salt and the puréed ginger; slit the green chilli in the middle and throw this in as well. Lower the heat, cover and cook for about 20-25 minutes or until the okra is tender.
3. Serve hot, garnished with fresh coriander.

143

DHAAL
Gingered red lentils

SERVES 6

275g/10oz masoor dal *(split red lentils)*
*1 teaspoon finely chopped fresh root
ginger*
1 teaspoon finely chopped garlic
salt

FOR THE *BAGHAAR*

75g/3oz unsalted butter
1 tablespoon onion seeds (kalongi)
1 tablespoon yellow mustard seeds
3 fresh or dried curry leaves
1 large onion, sliced
1 tomato, chopped
1 tablespoon freshly chopped coriander
2 teaspoons salt

1. Pick over and wash the lentils, then
soak in cold water for 1 hour.

2. Drain the water and rinse the lentils
again. Boil the lentils in 600ml/1pt
water with the ginger and garlic for
25-30 minutes or until the lentils are soft
enough to be mashed.

3. Remove the cooked lentils from the
heat and mash gently to a smooth paste,
adding more water if necessary. Season
to taste with salt.

4. For the *baghaar* dressing, melt the
butter and add the onion and mustard
seeds, and the curry leaves. Stir-fry
these for about 1 minute, then add the
chopped onion and tomato, fresh coriander and salt; continue stir-frying the
mixture for a further 2 minutes over a
low heat.

5. Remove the baghaar from the heat
and pour over the lentils. Serve hot.

Note:
¼ teaspoon of turmeric may also be
added to the lentils when boiling to add
a little colour.

CRUNCHY MOOLI SALAD

The unusual ingredient used in this
salad is mooli, or *daikon*, also known as
Japanese radish. Grown widely in Japan,
it does in fact come from the radish family
and has a similar taste to radish; it's very
popular in India and Pakistan.

SERVES 6

75g/3oz green pepper, seeded
100g/4oz cucumber
175g/6oz tomatoes
75g/3oz mooli
100g/4oz carrots
*100g/4oz chick peas, soaked overnight
and cooked*
2-3 tablespoons lemon juice
½ teaspoon salt
8 crisp lettuce leaves
*6-8 onion rings, 2 green chillies and 1
tablespoon freshly chopped coriander,
to garnish*
½ teaspoon sweet paprika

1. Dice the green pepper, cucumber,
tomatoes, mooli and carrots and mix
with the chick peas.

2. Mix the lemon juice and salt and
sprinkle over the vegetables.

3. Arrange the lettuce leaves on a plate.
Place the vegetables and chick peas on
the lettuce, garnish with onion rings, the
whole green chillies and fresh coriander,
and sprinkle the paprika over the top.

*Clockwise from left: bhindi; matar
pulao; masalay dar aloo; dhaal; and
crunchy mooli salad*

WINE NOTES

While most Indian vegetarians never drink wine (Shehzad Husain prefers chilled mango juice), there is no real reason why it should not accompany Indian food. India itself does make a sparkling wine (by the champagne method, no less) which is quite good enough to make seasonal celebrations fizz along nicely. Omar Khayyam Royal Mousseux (alias Marquise de Pompadour Royal Mousseux) is made by Shamrao Chougule's Indage group at a purpose-built winery at Narayangaon near Bombay, with advice and assistance from the Piper-Heidsieck champagne house. It is soft, flowery and delicately perfumed: challenge your local wine merchant to obtain supplies!

Meanwhile you can substitute any good sparkling wine. G. F. Cavalier Brut is a long-standing favourite, and Spanish Cava wines have improved beyond recognition in recent years. Other options would be tingling fresh Italian whites—Soave and Lugana are bland but accommodating; Bianco di Custoza or Vernaccia di San Gimignane have more character and class.

For red wine lovers, have a French vin de pays *or Beaujolais* nouveau—*this is not a meal for expensive fine wines. The fresher and fruitier your choice, the better you are likely to be pleased.*

KHEER
Indian rice pudding

Kheer is a very popular dessert, made on special occasions. *Varg* is finely beaten silver leaf, and can be bought at Indian supermarkets.

SERVES 6

100g/4oz basmati rice
6 green cardamoms, husks removed and seeds crushed
½ teaspoon saffron strands
1.2L/2pt milk
250g/8oz sugar
15g/½oz finely chopped unsalted pistachio nuts, 15g/½oz flaked almonds, and 1 piece varg, to garnish

1. Wash the basmati rice very thoroughly, then add the crushed cardamom seeds and the saffron strands. Add 700ml/1¼pt milk to the rice and bring to the boil.

2. Lower the heat, cover and simmer for about 45 minutes, stirring the mixture occasionally. Remove from the heat and mash the rice down well with a wooden spoon.

3. Add the sugar and stir well. Now add the remaining milk. Return the saucepan to a low heat and stir, then cover and simmer, stirring occasionally, for a further 10-12 minutes or until thickened.

4. Transfer the rice pudding to a serving dish and garnish. Serve it warm or cold.

Ken Hom

CHINESE NEW YEAR MENU

The Chinese New Year arrives with the appearance of the second new moon after 22 December – just in time to banish those post-Christmas blues. While traditionalists will enjoy 10-course banquets, Ken Hom's approach is lighter yet retains the spirit of the festivities

Fried aubergines with ginger salsa

Roasted poussins with rice wine sauce
Turnip and parsnip purée
Green salad

Coconut custard

For the Chinese, the New Year is a special time of intricate cultural rituals and family observations, most of which revolve around food, and my family was no exception. Because it is one of the most auspicious meals of the year, all the food served has symbolic meaning. For example, fish is the symbol of abundance, black moss seaweed means prosperity, while lotus roots and winter melon are eaten for marital harmony and growth. After the New Year's banquet each family is supposed to retire to its home and keep a wakeful, night-long vigil over the passing of the year.

There is an old belief that the New Year is a monster that might devour everyone should people not be awake to chase it away. Also, brooms are put away so that you will not sweep out good luck by mistake. Although customs vary from region to region, the celebrations continue after the first week until the 15th day of the month, when it all comes to an end with a lantern festival that is accompanied by rice flour dumplings, made into a round shape to represent the mid-month full moon. At that point, the holiday is over and everyone goes back to planning for the next year.

The different kinds of food served at Chinese New Year celebrations can vary from family to family. Purists insist nothing but vegetables should be eaten, but it has become a custom to have a 10-course banquet including many meats. All of this, of course, makes sense to the pragmatic Chinese. However, because of my partly Western upbringing, I tend to eschew the traditional forms of celebrations. I prefer a more re-laxed way of entertaining. Instead of making a strictly Chinese meal, I call my style of food 'East meets West'. It emphasizes the blending of food, spices, flavourings and techniques of Eastern and Western traditions.

I like to serve champagne with a first course because it is a festive way to begin an evening. The fried aubergines can be done in front of the guests while they are standing and enjoying their drinks. I think that watching freshly fried foods coming hot out of the pan or wok is a wonderful bit of entertainment, as

The day before
• *Make the coconut custard and chill. Dry-fry the coconut for decoration.*

In the morning
• *Make the turnip and parsnip purée.*

Two hours before dinner
• *Prepare the poussins and marinate for 1 hour.*
• *Prepare the ginger salsa.*

Half an hour before
• *Heat the oven to 200C/ 400F/gas 6. Roast the poussins for 30-40 minutes.*
• *Prepare the batter for the fried aubergines; leave it to stand for 20 minutes.*
• *Prepare the green salad and refrigerate.*

Just before the guests arrive
• *Start frying the aubergine slices, keeping each batch warm.*
• *Sprinkle the coconut over the custards.*

After the first course
• *Transfer roasted poussins to a warmed platter and make rice wine butter sauce.*
• *Reheat turnip and parsnip purée gently.*

well as a good ice-breaker.

Next come the roasted poussins. This easy-to-make dish captures a distinctive blend of colours, texture, and above all, flavours. The fine-textured meat is made succulent by an Eastern marinade. The sauce is made with butter (a Western touch), stock, Sichuan peppercorns, and rice wine. Pair this with the gingery turnip and parsnip purée to add a zesty note. A good claret would do this hearty dinner justice.

I like to follow the main course with a simple green salad which acts as a palate cleanser and inter-mission before the dessert. The coconut custard can, of course, be made ahead of time. I find it equally delicious hot or cold, served with delicate biscuits. With a sweet white wine or port it is an unusual ending to an enjoyable relaxed meal and an auspicious beginning for the New Year!

FRIED AUBERGINES WITH GINGER SALSA

SERVES 6

500g/1lb small aubergines
450ml/¾pt oil, preferably groundnut, otherwise sunflower
FOR THE BATTER
50g/2oz plain flour
½ teaspoon salt
FOR THE GINGER SALSA
400g/14oz fresh or canned tomatoes, skinned, seeded and chopped
1 tablespoon finely chopped spring onion
2 teaspoons finely chopped fresh ginger
1 teaspoon finely chopped garlic
2 tablespoons lime juice
2 teaspoons sugar
1 fresh chilli, seeded and finely chopped
2 tablespoons finely chopped fresh coriander
salt
freshly ground black pepper

1. Cut the aubergines into 4cm/1½in thick slices but do not peel them.

2. In a small bowl, mix the flour, salt and 150ml/¼pt water together and strain through a fine sieve. Allow the batter to rest for about 20 minutes.

3. Combine all the ingredients for the salsa and process for a few seconds in a food processor or blender. Season with salt and freshly ground pepper.

4. Heat the oil in a large wok or deep-fat fryer until the temperature reaches 190C/375F on a fat thermometer. Dip the slices of aubergine into the batter, drain the excess batter and deep fry them until crisp and golden brown. You may have to do this in several batches. Keep them warm in a low oven while frying the rest. Drain them well on crumpled kitchen paper. Serve at once with the sauce on the side.

Note:

If you don't own a fat thermometer, test the temperature of fat by dropping in a cube of bread. When the temperature reaches 190C/375F the cube of bread will brown in 50 seconds.

ROASTED POUSSINS WITH RICE WINE SAUCE

SERVES 6

3 × 700g/1½lb fresh poussins
FOR THE MARINADE
1¼ tablespoons light soy sauce
1¼ tablespoons dark soy sauce
3 tablespoons rice wine or dry sherry
1½ tablespoons sesame oil
FOR THE RICE WINE SAUCE
450ml/¾pt home-made chicken stock
200ml/7fl. oz rice wine or dry sherry
1½ tablespoons unroasted Sichuan peppercorns
40g/1½oz cold butter, cubed
3 tablespoons finely shredded spring onions, green part only, to garnish

1. Place the poussins on their breasts and cut down either side of the backbones and remove them. Turn over and flatten the birds by pressing down with the palm of your hand. Cut off the leg stumps and the third wing joints. Make two small holes in the skin near the end of the birds and tuck their legs through.

Dry them thoroughly on both sides with kitchen paper and place them, skin side up, in a large roasting tin.

2. In a small bowl mix the soy sauces, rice wine and sesame oil. Pour the mixture over the poussins, and rub it in well. Leave for 1 hour at room temperature.

3. Heat the oven to 200C/400F/gas 6. Roast the poussins, skin side up, in the marinade for 30-40 minutes or until the poussins are cooked. The juices should run yellow when the flesh is pierced. Baste the poussins occasionally.

4. Remove the birds from the roasting tin to a warmed platter. Skim off any fat and place the tin on the stove, adding the stock, rice wine and Sichuan peppercorns. Boil hard to reduce the liquid to about 225ml/8fl. oz. Strain out the peppercorns and save a few for garnish. Whisk in the butter, piece by piece, adding each one as the last melts.

5. To serve, cut the poussins in half and spoon a few tablespoons of sauce on to individual plates and place the poussin halves on top. Garnish with the spring onion strips and peppercorns.

TURNIP AND PARSNIP PURÉE

SERVES 6

500g/1lb turnips, cut up into large pieces
500g/1lb parsnips, cut up into large pieces
25g/1oz butter
1-1½ tablespoons finely chopped fresh ginger
3 tablespoons finely chopped spring onions, including the green parts
salt and black pepper
150ml/¼pt semi-skimmed milk

1. Cook the turnips and parsnips in lightly salted water until just tender, then purée them in a food processor or blender.
2. Heat the butter in a wok or frying pan and sauté the ginger and spring onions for 1 minute. Add the puréed vegetables, salt, freshly ground pepper and milk and cook for 5 minutes over low heat. Serve at once.

This dish can easily be reheated, but it must be done slowly to prevent scorching.

COCONUT CUSTARD

SERVES 6

4 size 3 eggs, beaten
100g/4oz caster sugar
400ml/14fl. oz canned coconut milk
¼ teaspoon salt
100g/4oz grated fresh or desiccated coconut

1. Heat the oven to 150C/300F/gas 2. Combine the eggs, sugar, coconut milk and salt in a large bowl and mix well.
2. Pour the custard mixture into 6 × 150ml/¼pt ramekins or an 850ml/1½pt baking dish. Place the ramekins or dish inside a large roasting tin. Pour hot water into it to come two-thirds of the way up the dish or ramekins.
3. Transfer the tin to the oven and bake for 35 minutes for the ramekins or 1 hour for the baking dish. Test if the custard is cooked by inserting the tip of a knife into the centre. If it is set, the blade will come out clean.
4. Allow to cool, then chill.
5. Dry fry the coconut, in a frying pan, until brown. Allow it to cool and sprinkle over the custard.

WINE NOTES

If you want to put out streamers to celebrate Chinese New Year, champagne is the way to do it. The Chinese do not stint when it comes to hospitality and entertainment!

Claret to go with Chinese food needs to be more than usually plump and generous. Normally I would probably recommend spicy, full-flavoured Gewürztraminer from Alsace to go with this food. But the succession of good vintages in Bordeaux means there is no shortage of good, easy-drinking clarets. Plump for something with more Merlot than Cabernet Sauvignon in its make-up, and ask a reliable wine merchant for a good fruity petit château wine and you should not be disappointed.

There are also some attractive spicy mouthfuls to be found among the wines from areas such as Côtes du Ventoux and the Côtes du Roussillon, and even among the improved wines now being produced in the French Midi.

For the dessert wine a really ripe raisin-fruity Muscat will be like adding a garnish of lip-smacking marmalade to the coconut custard. There are good examples from Spain and Australia as well as the south of France. Inscrutable they aren't.

151

Colin Spencer

VEGETARIAN VERVE

Take a break from wintery stodge and anticipate the coming of spring with Colin Spencer's simple, fresh-tasting menu

Herb bread
Smoked tofu kebabs with sesame sauce

Gratin vert with couscous pilaf and glazed parsnips

Syrian fruit salad with soft cheese

It is not difficult for a vegetarian to make a healthy slimming meal a gourmet one, too, as I hope this menu proves. It goes without saying, also, that food should look as appealing as it is appetizing to taste – which is one area in which vegetarian food, with its dependence on crisp, bright vegetables, scores an advantage over other recipes.

Tofu is high in protein and particularly valuable to vegetarians since, combined with grains, it provides an almost perfect balance of proteins (hence the couscous pilaf served with the main course).

The main course, gratin vert, is a favourite recipe of mine. Do experiment with hot avocado but be very careful that you just heat it through very gently – the flavour degenerates quickly with heat so it should never be cooked.

Clockwise from left: smoked tofu kebabs with sesame sauce; herb bread; glazed parsnips; Syrian fruit salad; gratin vert; and couscous pilaf

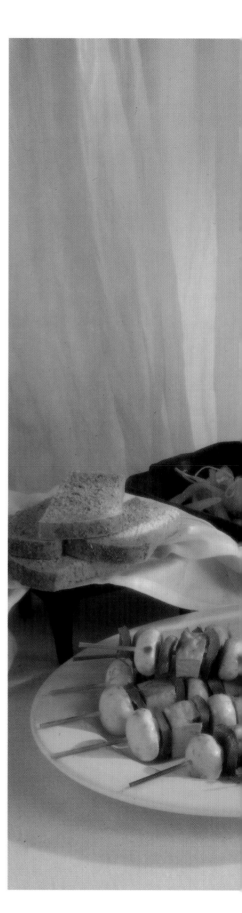

COUNTDOWN

The day before
- *Marinate the dried fruit.*
- *Marinate the tofu, mushrooms and peppers.*

Two hours before
- *Make the dough for the herb bread and leave it to rise.*
- *Add the remaining fruit to the fruit salad.*

One hour before
- *Bake the bread.*
- *Prepare the vegetables for the gratin.*

Just before
- *Prepare the parsnips and put them in the oven.*
- *Prepare and cook the couscous pilaf.*
- *Cook the kebabs and make the sauce.*

After the first course
- *Steam the vegetables, prepare the avocados, mix together in a gratin dish and grill.*
- *Reduce the cooking liquid from the parsnips and garnish them.*

After the main course
- *Top each fruit salad serving with soft cheese.*

I love to use grains other than rice, and couscous has a nutty flavour that complements the other dishes well. As for the glazed parsnips, this vegetable has natural sweetness which the glaze enhances.

Dried apricots have a high mineral and vitamin content, and this is why I have included them in this menu. They are perfect for the extravagantly rich-tasting fruit salad that finishes the meal.

HERB BREAD

MAKES 12 SLICES
250g/8oz wholemeal flour
250g/8oz strong white unbleached flour
1 teaspoon salt
2 tablespoons olive oil, plus extra for greasing
7g/¼oz sachet easy-blend dried yeast (with added vitamin C if possible)
1 teaspoon celery seeds, plus extra to garnish
1 teaspoon dill seeds, plus extra to garnish
1 teaspoon dried sage
200-225ml/7-8fl. oz warm water
beaten egg for glazing

1. Mix all the ingredients together, adding enough warm water to give a stiff, pliable dough; knead for 6-8 minutes if using dough hooks and 10 minutes if you are working by hand.
2. If you are going to use a bread tin (1L/2pt), grease it liberally and place the dough in it, cover with a clean cloth or cling film and leave in a warm place until it has increased in size to fill the tin (about 50-60 minutes). If you prefer not to use a tin, shape the dough and place it on a baking tray. Cover the dough with an upturned bowl.
3. Heat the oven to 220C/425F/gas 7 while the dough is proving. Glaze the loaf with beaten egg and sprinkle with celery and dill seeds. Bake the bread for 40-45 minutes until the underside sounds hollow when tapped. Serve the herb bread warm.

SMOKED TOFU KEBABS WITH SESAME SAUCE

SERVES 6
250g/8oz smoked tofu
250g/8oz button mushrooms
2 green peppers
3 tablespoons tahina
radicchio leaves, flat-leaved parsley and lime wedges to garnish
FOR THE MARINADE
juice and grated zest of 2 large limes
25g/1oz grated ginger root
sea salt
freshly ground black pepper

1. Cube the tofu, cutting 4-5 cubes per person, then delicately score each piece on two sides, diagonally. Wipe the mushrooms and remove their stalks. Core, seed and cube the peppers.
2. Combine the marinade ingredients. Add the tofu, mushrooms and peppers and leave them all to marinate for 24 hours.
3. Drain the tofu and vegetables and arrange alternately on 6 skewers; reserve the marinade for the sesame sauce. Then place the skewers under a hot grill until the tofu is sizzling and just brown at the edges.
4. Meanwhile, make the sauce by mixing the tahina with 2 tablespoons water and the reserved marinade. Taste and then check the seasoning.
5. To serve, arrange the kebabs on plates, garnish with radicchio, flat-leaved parsley and lime wedges and serve with the tahina and marinade sauce.

Note:
Tofu is made from soya beans, so you might almost call it a vegetable cheese. It's sold in soft-textured white cubes. Look for smoked tofu in the chilled cabinets of most health food shops and Chinese groceries and supermarkets.

COUSCOUS PILAF

SERVES 6
175g/6oz couscous
3 garlic cloves, crushed
3-4 tender celery stalks, finely chopped, leaves reserved for garnish
500g/1lb carrots, grated or pared into long strips
sea salt
freshly ground black pepper

1. Place the couscous in a metal colander standing over a saucepan and pour boiling water over it. Leave for 20 minutes, separating the grains with your fingers so that lumps do not form.
2. Stir in the garlic, celery and carrot. Steam for 20 minutes. Season lightly and serve, garnished with celery leaves.

GRATIN VERT

SERVES 6
1kg/2lb broccoli or calabrese
1kg/2lb small courgettes
1kg/2lb slender leeks
25g/1oz butter
2 ripe avocados
handful of parsley, finely chopped
juice and grated zest of 1 lemon
sea salt
pinch of white pepper

1. Cut the florets from the broccoli or calabrese. Remove the hard outer layer of the stalks with a potato peeler.
2. Slice the courgettes diagonally into 2.5cm/1in lengths. Do the same with the leeks, washing them thoroughly in the process.
3. Steam all the vegetables for 5-8 minutes until tender but still with some bite. Melt the butter in a large, flameproof gratin dish and add the vegetables.
4. Peel and stone the avocados, slice them carefully and add them to the dish. Sprinkle over half of the parsley with the lemon zest and juice, and season. Cook for a minute or two, taking care that the vegetables don't overcook.
5. Place the dish under a pre-heated

grill for a few moments to heat the avocado through – but do not let it cook – then sprinkle with the remaining parsley and serve.

GLAZED PARSNIPS

SERVES 6
1kg/2lb small parsnips
300ml/½pt fresh orange juice
2 tablespoons grated orange zest
2 tablespoons redcurrant jelly
sea salt
freshly ground black pepper
blanched julienne strips of orange rind to garnish

1. Heat the oven to 200C/400F/gas 6. Trim, peel and quarter the parsnips and place them in a shallow ovenproof dish. Heat the orange juice with the zest and melt the redcurrant jelly in it. Season and pour over the prepared parsnips.
2. Cover and bake for 20-25 minutes until tender. Pour off the liquid and reduce to about 2 tablespoons by boiling hard. Pour over the parsnips and serve, garnished with strips of orange rind.

SYRIAN FRUIT SALAD WITH SOFT CHEESE

SERVES 6
75g/3oz dried apricots
50g/2oz dried pears
50g/2oz dried apple rings
50g/2oz dried figs
450ml/¾pt apple juice
2 clementines or satsumas
6 fresh or canned lychees
100g/4oz low-fat soft cheese (quark or fromage frais) to serve

1. Roughly chop the dried fruit and place in a large glass bowl. Pour over the apple juice and leave to marinate overnight.
2. Peel and segment the clementines or satsumas and peel the lychees. Add both to the dried fruit. Serve, topping each portion with a spoonful of the soft cheese.

WINE NOTES

This is the sort of menu most likely to appeal to those who are apt to search for organic products, and who might buy self-professedly 'organic' wines. As far as wine is concerned, though, bear in mind that many of the best producers already follow organic principles and methods without requiring to pay for affiliation to an organic association which will encourage them to boast about the fact.

Unfortunately, no wines (not even organic ones) are made without some additives and processing: if they were, they would be vinegars, not wines. My own notions with this meal would be a smoky California Fumé Blanc (Robert Mondavi is ultra-reliable) to start, and a spicy, herby Côtes du Rhône, Lirac or Côtes du Ventoux to follow. François Perrin's Cru du Coudelet, for example, is a Côtes du Rhone so good that it is practically Châteauneuf-du-Pape, and it is made by impeccable organic methods—even if it does not say so on the label.

BIOGRAPHIES

Suzy Benghiat
Born and brought up in Cairo, Suzy Benghiat moved to Britain in 1948. Author of *Middle Eastern Cookery*, she runs courses on cooking her native food, and has taught at Kenneth Lo's school and at Leith's.

Frances Bissell
Winner of the Observer/Mouton Cadet Dinner Party Competition in 1983, Frances Bissell has written *A Cook's Calendar* and *The Pleasures of Cookery* and is the food correspondent on *The Times*.

Sonia Blech
Sonia Blech is the chef/proprietor of the Restaurant Mijanou in Pimlico — favourite restaurant of *Times* columnist Bernard Levin.

Maddalena Bonino
Brought up in the Piedmont region of Italy, Maddalena Bonino won the coveted Observer/Mouton Cadet Competition in 1987. Now a chef at Frith's Restaurant, Soho, she is a regular writer for Time-Life.

Giuliano Bugialli
Guliano Bugialli divides his time teaching at his two cookery schools in Florence and New York, besides lecturing and demonstrating all over the world. He is author of *A Taste of Italy*.

Antonio Carluccio
Formerly a wine merchant, Antonio Carluccio took over the Neal Street Restaurant in 1981. Passionate about producing authentic Italian food, his is also the only restaurant offering up to fifteen different types of wild mushroom in season.

Glynn Christian
Glynn Christian appears twice a week on BBC's 'Breakfast Time', besides running his own cookery centre in London. A founder member of The Guild of Food Writers, he is the author of several books.

Josceline Dimbleby
Brought up in South America and the Middle East, Josceline Dimbleby has written numerous very successful cookery books including the best-selling *Favourite Food* and the popular series for Sainsbury's. She is a regular contributor to magazines and to the Sunday Telegraph.

Coralie Dorman
A professional cook, contributor to many books and magazines, and former Cookery Editor of *Taste*, Coralie Dorman is now a freelance writer.

Canon John Eley
The son of a shepherd, John Eley, *The Cooking Canon* (the title of his latest book), took up cooking as a child. Now a Canon at Bromsgrove, Worcestershire, he is also the author — with Lionel Blue — of the best-selling *Simply Divine*.

Clare Ferguson
Clare Ferguson was born and educated in New Zealand, where she began her career in food. Now a noted writer, food stylist and food consultant in Great Britain as well, she has written several books, most recently *Gourmet Microwave Cookery*.

Lyn Hall
On coming to Britain from South Africa in 1970 Lyn Hall became a restaurant manager. After cooking in several 3-star restaurants, she opened her own school, *La Petite Cuisine*, in 1976, and now also runs a food consultancy, Cuisine Creative.

Ken Hom
Star of the popular television series 'Chinese Cookery', Ken Hom was born in the USA of Cantonese parents. He began to learn the art of Chinese cooking at the age of 11, working part-time in his uncle's restaurant, and he has been a food consultant and teacher worldwide since 1974.

Shehzad Husain
Besides teaching cookery, Shehzad Husain is the author of many books on Indian and Pakistani food. Particularly concerned with preserving the authentic tastes of her native cuisine while introducing it to a wider audience, she is now consultant to Marks & Spencer on their Indian range of foods.

Lisa Kinsman
A fashion model and interior designer who has lived in England since the 1960s, Lisa Kinsman — born in Hong Kong — has not lost her love of Chinese food. A fine cook herself, she was also the presenter of a television programme on Chinese cookery.

Antony Kwok
A fashion designer from Hong Kong, Antony Kwok is also a very skilled cook whose awards include the London Standard Gastronomic Seafish Cook of 1986, and runner-up in the Observer/Mouton Cadet Menu Competition.

Ann Long
A professional chef, Ann Long is one of the few women members of the International Master Chefs Institute. She runs the Oakhill House Restaurant near Bath, Avon, with her husband and daughter, and has written a book on dinner party entertaining.

Fay Maschler
Fay Maschler gained a faithful following of thousands with her restaurant reviews and then her cookery column for *The Evening Standard*. She is the author of the *Guide to Eating out in London* (1986), and she recently presented the popular television series 'Teaching Your Child to Cook'.

Bonnie Rabert
Bonnie Rabert was for fifteen years a food consultant in the United States. She lived for a time in Britain before returning to her native Chicago, where she now specializes in food styling for photography and recipe development.

Harvey Sambrook
Harvey Sambrook has lived in France, Spain and Sardinia, where he opened his first restaurant in 1969. After nearly 20 years as a restaurateur, he now writes about travel and food.

Colin Spencer
Novelist, playwright and artist, Colin Spencer now devotes most of his time to food writing, with a column on *The Guardian* and many books to his name, including *Cordon Vert* and *The Romantic Vegetarian*.

Caroline Waldegrave
After training at the Cordon Bleu School in London, Caroline Waldegrave studied further in the USA, and is now co-principal of Leith's School of Food and Wine.

Hilary Walden
Formerly a food technologist, Hilary Walden now specializes in writing about food, wine and restaurants. A regular contributor to many magazines and newspapers, she has also written 20 books, including *The Steaming Cook Book* and *Pâtisserie of France*.

Robin Young
A founder member of The British Gastronomic Academy, Robin Young's interest in wine started with a holiday job in a wine cellar. Now a reporter on *The Times*, he writes a regular wine column for *The Decanter* and is Wine Editor of *Taste*.

INDEX

Page numbers in italics refer to illustrations

PICTURE ACKNOWLEDGMENTS

Page 8 Jan Baldwin; 10 Jim Forest; 11, 13 Peter Myers; 16 BEAP Ltd; 17, 18-19, 20-21 Jan Baldwin; 22, 23, 24-25, 26 Grant Symon; 27 BEAP Ltd; 28, 30-31, 32, 33 Martin Brigdale; 34-35, 37, 38-39, 40 BEAP Ltd; 41 Trevor Leighton; 42-43 Alan Newnham; 46 Grant Symon; 48, 49 Martin Brigdale; 50, 52 BEAP Ltd; 54 Martin Brigdale; 55, 57, 58, 59 John Hollingshead; 60 BEAP Ltd; 61, 62, 63, 64, 65 Grant Symon; 66 BEAP Ltd; 67, 70 Peter Myers; 72 BEAP Ltd; 73 John Hollingshead; 76, 77 BEAP Ltd; 78, 79, 81, 82, 83, 84 Alan Newnham; 85, 86-87, 88, 89 Martin Brigdale; 90 Marshall Cavendish Ltd; 92, 94-95, 96-97 Vernon Morgan; 98 © 1984 John Dominis; 102, 103 Martin Brigdale; 104, 105, 106-107, 108 John Hollingshead; 109, 111, 112, 113, 114 Marshall Cavendish Ltd; 116-117 Alan Newnham; 120 BEAP Ltd; 122, 123, 124, 125, 126, 127 Laurie Evans; 128, 129, 130-131, 133 Alan Newnham; 134, 135, 136, 138-9, 140 BEAP Ltd; 141, 142, 144-145, 146 John Hollingshead; 148, 149, 150, 151 Jan Baldwin; 152 Trevor Leighton; 153 Alan Newnham.